GREAT WESTERN STEAM in the West Country

GREAT WESTERN
STEAM IN THE WEST COUNTRY

edited by '4588'

D. BRADFORD BARTON LTD

Frontispiece: Exeter (St. Davids), 26 September 1959, with the down 'Cornish Riviera' passing through behind No.6995 *Benthall Hall,* of Taunton, and ailing 'Warship' D601 *Ark Royal.* Almost three-quarters of an hour behind schedule, the 'Halls' crew have little chance of making up the lost time before they reach Newton Abbot where doubtless there will be a change to new engines. Nevertheless they are not far from the 55 mph speed limit on the down through road after the long fast run down from the summit of Wellington bank. On the right at Platform 1 is a local waiting to leave for Kingswear, behind 2-6-2T No.5524 from Exeter shed. This stopping train has been held, to avoid further delay to the Riviera.

[P. Q. Treloar]

© Copyright D. Bradford Barton Ltd ISBN 085153 2888

Published by Enterprise Transport Books Ltd
3 Barnsway, Kings Langley, Hertfordshire WD4 9PW

Printed and bound in Great Britain by BPC Hazell Books Ltd

introduction

A sub-title for this volume might well be added 'in the final decade of steam' for it does cover only the years from the early 1950s onwards and not those when the GWR was a company rather than a Region. Subsequent volumes in this Great Western Steam series will cover this earlier period, to present the whole picture over the years.

This volume commences at Exeter and proceeds westward to Penzance. It might be argued that there is more to the West Country than lies west of Exeter but nevertheless this is the chosen starting point. Newton Abbot, where Torbay/Cornwall trains divided or combined is a typical division point – particularly as the famous 'banks' start west of here – but this would have meant omitting the coastal line through Dawlish and Teignmouth. Much of interest has had to be left out, or perhaps held over for a sequel in due course. As there have already been two volumes in the series on Cornwall as well as on Devon, the opportunity has been taken to put the accent in the captions herein on the operational aspect of train working in the West Country – permitted loads, sidings, bankers, special traffic and the like. Ocean Liner specials, Kingswear coal trains, Saltash auto-trains, broccoli specials, Austerities at Aller, and the Newton breakdown train show how wide the variety of workings was – quite apart from such everyday scenes as doubleheaders, milk trains and long distance freights. Primarily it is the main line, plus the Torbay/Kingswear 'branch' that is covered, for branch lines are another separate subject due for individual treatment within the 'Great Western Steam' series.

It is a tribute to the immense interest and variety of train working between Exeter and Penzance – no more than 131 route miles – that a fifth volume on them should still be of interest and should still enable one to show so much that is new. And it is interesting to reflect that before publication of the Great Western Steam series, not one single pictorial volume on this West Country scene had appeared . . . .

The West Country could lay claim to having perhaps the most difficult busy main line of any in Britain; nothing in any way comparable to it on the LNER or Southern, whilst on the LMS there was the long 1 in 100 of the Settle-Carlisle route and the 1 in 75 of Shap. But compare this with 1 in 37, which locomotive engineers everywhere know is not a simple matter of being arithmetically twice as steep . . . . Dainton and Hemerdon were both on this daunting gradient whilst innumerable stretches of 1 in 60 or worse occurred everywhere between Aller Junction and Hayle, allied to curves of far worse severity than anything on the LMSR main line to Scotland. Small wonder the Great Western was never a line for Pacifics, preferring every spare pound of tractive weight on the banks coming back on to coupled drivers and not on to a trailing truck.

From time to time, a Southern West Country Pacific might be seen working along the WR main line west of Newton, and drivers had to handle even their reduced loads gingerly to avoid 'dancing' displays such as a 'Castle' driver never thought of. It is curious, too, in considering these steep grades, that the area is not mountainous – terrain that one normally associates with severe climbs. Yet the soft South Devon countryside and its Cornish counterpart threw up the most formidable inclines anywhere on British double-tracked main line.

'4588' is the *nom-de-plume* of two Westcountrymen, one from Devon and one from Cornwall, whose memories of Great Western steam at work in the West Country are both fond and wide-ranging. This 2-6-2T was for many years a favourite at sheds in the area and now lives on, after the era of main line steam has gone, on the Dart Valley Railway Company's two lines.

No.5072 *Hurricane* eases 'The Royal Duchy' over to the platform line opposite Exeter Middle box at the north end of St. Davids, ready for the stop. This express, 1.30 off Paddington, was named in January 1957 and ran to Penzance. In the foreground of this illustration can be seen the spur, ending at the buffer stops, where the Southern banking engines waited between turns of duty helping up the 1 in 37 climb to Exeter Central; 28 August 1957. [A. R. Butcher]

Most photography in the West Country dates from the summer months; as something of a change from the usual warm sunshine enjoyed by holidaying photographers, is a scene in mid-winter, with No.6008 *King James II* on the up 'Limited' on a January day in 1959. A little time usually lost on the banks between Plymouth and Newton, or in detaching the pilot at the latter, but two minutes recovery time were allowed on each side of White Ball summit and it was rare for this, the principal West of England express, to be other than dead on time through Taunton in the up direction. [P. Q. Treloar]

'Castle' No.5058 *Earl of Clancarty* passing through Exeter St. Thomas station on 9 September 1961 with the 12.40 a.m. s.o. Newquay to Cardiff – reporting code T41, as chalked on the smokebox door. The typical Brunel-designed overall roof dated back to 1846 and has now been entirely demolished. Exeter at one time had no less than six stations. [W. L. Underhay]

A rural scene a few miles from Exeter on the Teign Valley line, between Christow and Ashton, with 2-6-2T No.4553 heading for Heathfield on 7 April 1958. This line, single track throughout, left the main line at City Basin Junction and provided a useful relief route to Newton Abbot as an alternative to the main line along the coast. The heaviest classes permitted except under emergency conditions, were 'Manors' (at a restricted 25 mph speed) but in BR days the Southern route via Okehampton was usually used in emergencies. [J. R. Besley]

Rail services in Devon and other parts of the West Country were seriously disrupted by flooding in March 1961 and the Teign Valley line was washed out at the locality seen above by the flooding of the Teign. By this date the route Exeter-Christow section had been closed completely and the rest retained for goods traffic only and this wash-out closed it east of Trusham. [J. R. Besley]

Heathfield station with 2-6-2T No.5168 entering on a Moretonhampstead train and passing beneath the narrow overbridge carrying the erstwhile A38 main road. This was the junction between the Teign Valley line and the Moretonhampstead branch running north from Newton Abbot. The line on the right led to the private siding of a works producing clay pipes etc.

[P. Q. Treloar]

No.5168 with a two coach train of non-corridor stock at the Mortonhampstead terminus. At this time of year the station is deserted but in summer it would be rather busier with ramblers and other visitors to Dartmoor, for this branch was quite well patronised in the era before such widespread ownership of cars. In fact passenger traffic ceased in March 1959. The overall wooden roof to the station was a notable feature.

[P. Q. Treloar]

In the summers of 1959-61 it was possible to see BR Standard 9F 2-10-0s on passenger turns in South Devon, as typified by this unidentified member of the class heading a Saturdays-only down train along the side of the Exe estuary near Starcross in September 1960. Many were from South Wales – being available for passenger duties at the weekend – as with this one hailing from Ebbw Junction, and heading the 9.05 a.m. Swansea to Kingswear.

[W. L. Underhay]

Shadows lengthen across Dawlish Warren station on an evening early in September 1957: No.7029 *Clun Castle* is going well on the through road with a twelve-coach down express and is bound home for Newton Abbot shed. The long running loops here, as well as serving the platforms, were of considerable advantage for operational reasons and enabled through trains to overtake freights or those due to stop. The station is still open today, serving the adjoining holiday camps and beaches. An interesting privately-owned museum has been established in the station building of the up platform.

[A. R. Butcher]

No.6003 *King George IV* with the 1.20 p.m. Penzance-Paddington at speed round the curve towards Dawlish Warren on 3 September 1960. At this point, having come through the cutting at the easternmost end of the Dawlish sea cliffs the line swings north to follow the side of the Exe estuary towards Exeter – a real racing stretch where the 75 mph speed limit was held for mile after mile. Erosion of the soft sandy shore was an incipient problem here and massive stone blocks have been dumped along the high water mark, alongside the footpath, to protect the main line.   [W. L. Underhay]

28xxs were not uncommon on heavier freight turns into or out of south Devon, although none were shedded nearer than Bristol. Exceptionally, too, one might be seen on a summer Saturday helping out a relief passenger working. They were allowed to work beyond Keyham and over the Royal Albert Bridge at Saltash, but were rarely seen west of Tavistock Junction. Here, No.2892 from Cardiff (Canton), is heading eastbound with a freight from Hackney yard at Newton Abbot, on 25 August 1957. She is in the cutting seen opposite and in the distance can be seen the buildings of Dawlish.   [A. R. Butcher]

With an immaculate rake of fourteen well-filled chocolate-and-cream liveried coaches behind the tender of No.6004 *King George III*, 'The Mayflower' makes an impressive sight sweeping east along the tracks bordering Dawlish sea-front. Consisting of a main Plymouth portion, to which a further set of coaches from Kingswear were added at Newton Abbot, this was a regular turn for Old Oak or Laira 'Kings'. Note the distinctive red sandstone cliffs bordering the line, with their curious pattern of erosion marks.   [A. R. Butcher]

No.4991 *Cobham Hall* restarts a down local away from Dawlish on 10 September 1957, bound for Kingswear. A rain shower, still visible over the sea, has wet the rails but she makes the usual surefooted start of a well-handled 'Hall'. Note the down starter, positioned on the landward side to give better visibility to drivers on the curve through the station, also the top of the girderwork forming the Colonnade Viaduct, 39 yards in length, which the locomotive is crossing.   [A. R. Butcher]

Another scene at Dawlish with 'Castle' Class No.5079 *Lysander* pulling away with the up Kingswear portion of 'The Cornishman' – and showing signs that both sets of cylinder glands need repacking. On the right, by the water tank, can be seen mile post 206, this distance being measured via Bristol. Direct it is 185¾ miles to Paddington. Dawlish had the not entirely enviable record of being the station nearest the sea on the GWR and high spring tides combined with onshore gales caused spray and seawater to break over the down platform. At such times as an emergency measure the up platform alone was used. Originally the platform, which overhangs the promenade, was built of sleepers and even without a gale, the splashing of waves at high tide could send water up to soak the legs of waiting passengers. On this score it was asphalted in the late 1950s. The platform has been seriously damaged in gales from time to time and its exposed position makes it a continuing problem to the railway authorities.

[A. R. Butcher]

No.5919 *Worsley Hall* passing Parsons Tunnel Signal Box, with a down train from Bristol on 10 September 1957. This box was normally operational on Saturdays only in the summer to provide intermediate control between Dawlish and Teignmouth boxes at the times when occupation of the line was so busy. In the days of steam there were something like a score of signal boxes in the twenty miles or so between Exeter and Aller Junction, half of them open continuously. The one seen here came into use in 1934 and finally closed in 1964.   [A. R. Butcher]

A down mixed goods behind 28xx No.2807 heads alongside the Teign estuary at high water after having passed the station and docks, September 1959. A considerable amount of masonry work in the many cuttings by the station and in the buttressed retaining wall here is an enduring local feature, in south Devon limestone.

[Derek Cross]

The driver of No.6005 *King George II* has the regulator shut and the blower on before running into the tunnel by Parsons Tunnel box with a Penzance-Paddington relief on a July Saturday in 1951. A variety of elderly coaching stock makes up the train, which at fifteen bogies, is near the 530-ton standard load for a 'King' east of Newton. In the foreground, some sizeable rockery stone keeps the sea at bay, placed here by the GWR in the 1880s when this section of line was doubled. This point is the start of the sea-wall which extends for well over a mile to Teignmouth, built of massive limestone masonry in-filled with rubble on a broad ledge that not only carries the tracks but also provides as firm a foundation as possible for the near-vertical 200' face of the cliff face on the landward side.

[Derek Cross]

The 1.20 p.m. Paddington to Kingswear occasionally produce a 47xx, and is seen here alongside the Teign estuary travelling towards Newton Abbot on 15 July 1961 with No.4704 in charge. On passenger trains, the 47xxs were restricted to 60 mph maximum speed.　　　[W. L. Underhay]

A photograph taken across the River Teign at the up end of Newton Abbot station, with No.4079 *Pendennis Castle* drawing away on 17 April 1961 with 'The Cornishman' bound for Wolverhampton. Three coaches from Kingswear have been added here to those of the original Penzance portion. 2-8-0 No.3841 is on the down goods line by Hackney yard which lies to the right. In the 1950s this important goods yard had four steam shunters employed round the clock on weekdays and numerous South Devon freights were assembled or broken here. To set back into the sidings, arriving goods trains had to draw right up over the bridge to clear the points before setting back. Six reception roads were provided and a fan of 22 main sidings.   [J. R. Besley]

A general view of Newton Abbot station from the east, with No.4955 *Plaspower Hall* departing for Exeter, August 1957. Originally the station had an all-over roof which was replaced in 1925-27 with the re-modelled layout as seen here. The through lines run on either side of the station and scissors crossovers were provided to help expedite the dividing of joining of the many trains which were for the Torbay line or destined for Plymouth. [A. R. Butcher]   Below, the west end of Newton, showing the locomotive shed and works behind, 4 April 1958. Apart from other local and main line duties, Newton Abbot m.p.d. covered the workings of the Kingswear 'branch' which possessed no other shed. The trio of locomotives prominent are No.5024 *Carew Castle,* No.4936 *Kinlet Hall* and No.2800.   [J. R. Besley]

No.6982 *Melmerby Hall* and No.5906 *Lawton Hall* make a vigorous start out of Newton Abbot on 10 April 1961 with the down 'Limited'. It was commonplace for a pair of 'Halls' to take over here on Saturdays in summer, or at Plymouth at other times, but on this occasion the train engine from Paddington, a 'Warship', had failed and the two 'Halls' had come through from some point farther east with the banks, curves and speed restrictions ahead, there is no possibility of hard running to bring the train back to its booked time. The permitted combined load limit for two 'Halls' west of here is 550 tons.

[J. R. Besley]

One of the last of the famous 'Plymouth Ocean Specials', run in connection with trans-Atlantic liners calling in Plymouth Sound to land passengers, was on 19 June 1961 when No.5029 *Nunney Castle* worked a train from Millbay to Paddington to convey passengers from a French Line vessel. The run, as usual, was non-stop apart from a halt outside Newton to detach the pilot, which in this case had been No.6863 *Dolhywel Grange*. The total load was thirteen vehicles, including five of the GWR special saloons earmarked for this service, plus normal 1st class dining cars and coaches etc. In the immediate postwar years on average of two or three up trains were run a week but very many fewer in the down direction. The number of trains run depended not only on the number of liners calling but whether the number of passengers to be landed – and to some extent their status – warranted a separate train with de-luxe accommodation. Some very fast times were put up by these 'Ocean Liner Specials', including a run in 3 hours 37 minutes in 1954.

[J. R. Besley]

2-8-2T No.7250 with Class H freight leaving Newton Abbot on the down relief line bound for Tavistock Junction 20 May, 1952. Newton shed had a few of this class at this period, one of their duties being to work trains of coal landed at Kingswear up to Torquay gas works.

[J. R. Besley]

Heading along the section of quadruple track leading to Aller Junction, 2-8-0 No.4706 is bound for Tavistock Junction yard with a freight on 5 March 1962. The first section of the train is composed of 'Herring' ballast hoppers destined for the quarries at Menheniot in Cornwall. The routes controlled by the fine GWR bracket signal reading from left to right are the Down Main (to Plymouth), the Aller Junction goods loop (where No.4706 will wait for banking assistance up Dainton), and the Torbay-Kingswear branch. Maximum load for the 47xx class over Dainton was 30 loaded or 40 empties; in practice bank engines were provided for almost all freight trains.   [J. R. Besley]

24

Another westbound freight, behind No.3848, plodding down the relief line at the same location on 22 August the same year. In the intervening months the down main has been re-laid and a colour-light bracket signal installed to control the up lines. The GWR semaphores in the foreground were also replaced later the same year by a more modern semaphore gantry. [J. R. Besley]

No.3848, with the same partly-fitted freight already illustrated, picks its route across the actual junction by Aller signal box and will run into the loop where a D63xx diesel-hydraulic is waiting to assist as banker. Just visible by the latter is the conical water tower used for supplying the bankers in steam days – normally 51xx tanks. The goods loop here, laid in during 1941 to cope with extra wartime traffic had nominal capacity for a 64 wagon train but the normal maximum load permitted up Dainton was 55 ten-tonners or their equivalent. 550 ton trains on a 1 in 37 stretch of busy mainline was rare if not unique in Britain; so far as is known the accident-free record of Dainton remains unblemished to this day.   [J. R. Besley]

No.6870 *Bodicote Grange* and No.5940 *Whitbourne Hall* pass the goods loop signals and prepare to start the four-mile climb up past Stoneycombe to Dainton Summit, September 1959. The great majority of long distance passenger trains from Newton to Plymouth were doubleheaded.

[Derek Cross]

The WD Class 2-8-0s were becoming rare in the West Country by 1960 but still wandered there from time to time from their usual haunts in South Wales. No.90676, from Ebbw Junction shed, exerts all her 34,000 lbs-odd of tractive effort in bringing a freight out of the loop, assisted in the rear by a 63xx diesel, 6 May 1961. A 28 minute margin was allowed for before Aller Junction signal box would allow a freight to proceed up Dainton, to avoid delay to a following express; hardly surprising, freights were extremely rare in South Devon in daylight hours when passenger traffic was heavy on summer Saturdays.

[W. L. Underhay]

Newton Abbot depot's big breakdown crane, No.3, together with a smaller twelve ton steam crane and its match truck, pulling out of Aller loop in September 1960 headed by No.4934 *Hindlip Hall*. The weight of the train, about 250 tons, is within load limit for a 'Hall' but, being unfitted, a banking 51xx is provided in the rear as a precautionary measure as far as Dainton Summit. The larger crane had a 36 ton lifting capacity and is seen en route to an engineering assignment rather than a derailment. In the middle of the train is a chain truck, necessary in the days when heavy steel chains were used for lifting in the days prior to light-weight steel hawsers. Bringing up the rear is a Dean carriage of 1900 vintage converted for use as a Mess and Tool Van for the train, and now on the Dart Valley Railway.

[W. L. Underhay]

A feature of summer Saturday operation on the busy Torquay and Kingswear line in steam days was the build-up of locomotives at Paignton from down expresses. Due to the difficulty of finding a path back for them in the already congested timetable, they were sent back to Newton Abbot in strings as and when they could be fitted in. There they were coaled, watered and turned ready for working back up-country. As many as five were permitted coupled together light between Paignton and Newton Abbot. Here, No.5043 *Earl of Mount Edgcumbe,* No.5981 *Frensham Hall* and No.5011 *Tintagel Castle* are en route for the shed on 12 August 1961. Aller Junction signal box is in the background. This dates from 1925, replacing an earlier box situated in the junction of the running lines, at a time when various other track layout improvements were carried out here.   [W. L. Underhay]

29

No.5999 *Wollaton Hall* trails a wintry exhaust across the fields near Kingskerswell with the Torquay portion of the 9.00 a.m. Wolverhampton-Penzance on 31 December 1960. [W. L. Underhay]

'Torre for St. Marychurch and Babbacombe' reads the station nameboard, familiar over the years to tens of thousands of GWR travellers and holidaymakers. This neat and well kept station lies on a brief easier stretch punctuating the otherwise severe climb up from Torquay towards Aller. Waiting in the station is No.5992 *Horton Hall* and the 1.35 p.m. from Exeter (St. Davids)-Kingswear which at this date (30 August 1962) consisted of through coaches off the 'Limited'. Note the elevated signal box on the left, built in this style in order that trains could be seen clearly on the steep climb from Torquay. [J. R. Besley]

Newton Abbots 51xx tanks were the maids-of-all-work on local and banking turns, with eight of the class allocated there in the 1950s. They handled most of the locals on the Kingswear line, as with No.4150 seen on the 1 in 73 of Torre bank with the 8.35 a.m. Kingswear-Newton Abbot, 25 June 1962. The first two non-corridor coaches of this mainly conveyed school-children; the other three are destined for Paddington and will be combined with 'The Mayflower' from Plymouth. These 51xx tanks normally faced in the down direction as here, working up trains bunker first. [J. R. Besley]

During a period of diesel shortage in February 1962, which coincided with a spell of wintry weather even in South Devon, steam came back to work the 'Devonian' between Paignton and Bristol. No.5055 *Earl of Eldon* blasts under the road bridge by the station with the up train on the last day of that month, in place of the customary 'Warship' diesel. Without assistance up the 1 in 55 here, a 'Castle' was permitted only eleven on, and over this was allowed 455 tons (= 14 bogies) if banked away as far as Torre advance starter. On a day like this, some sensitive handling of the regulator will be needed if *Earl of Eldon* is not to slip. [J. R. Besley]

No.4975 *Umberslade Hall* coasting down Torre bank towards Torquay with brakes on to keep speed within the 45 mph restriction and also achieve a smooth stop at the platform. The train is the overnight 11.32 p.m. from Manchester (Victoria) to Paignton on **8** July 1961, one which ran from June to August only. Below, No.4086 *Builth Castle* leaving Torquay on the climb up the 1 in 55 for the first mile or so away from the station with the 8.30 a.m. Kingswear to Newton Abbot (and Paddington) on 25 May 1961. [J. R. Besley]   33

The Kingswear line was hardly a branch at all, although technically classed as such compared to the main line on to Plymouth. It was classed as a Double Red route, and saw the 60xx class occasionally. 1962 was the last year before they were well and truly displaced by the new diesels and on 19 June No.6029 *King Edward VIII* had charge of the up 'Devonian'. The fireman has built up a full head of steam and the starter is down . . . .   [J. R. Besley]

Until its closing years, the gas works at Torquay, set on a site overlooking Hollacombe beach, was supplied with coal landed at Kingswear quay from coasters and brought up from there by rail. A variety of motive power handled this traffic over the years including the 51xx 2-6-2Ts. In this scene No.4174 is engaged in shunting coal empties in the sidings on 21 March 1961, having left the brake van standing on the down running line. The signal box here, like various others in South Devon, was switched in on busy summer Saturdays and on Bank Holidays to create an extra block section. Officially known as Gas House Siding Signal Box, it was opened for use in 1910 and was closed in 1966.
[J. R. Besley]

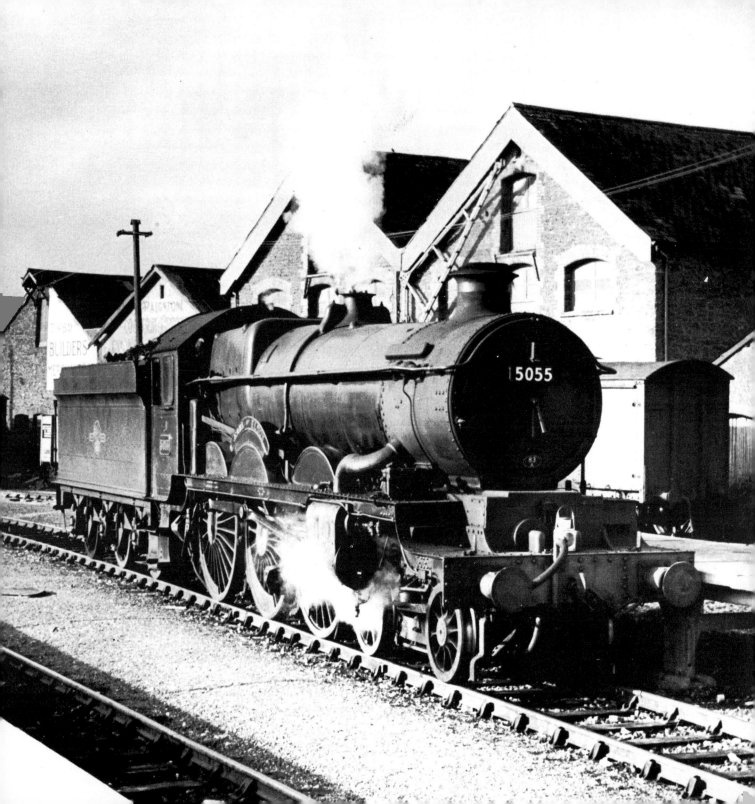

'Castle' class No.5055 *Earl of Eldon* in Paignton station yard, 21 September 1962. This was the last day a Newton Abbot engine worked here, No.5055 arrived on the morning goods from Hackney yard, and after turning at Goodrington and shunting, left for the return to Newton about noon. [J. R. Besley]

A special occasion for one of Newton Abbot's 51xx tanks, No.5153, on 30 March 1962 – working the through carriages off the 2.30 p.m. from Paddington which carried H.R.H. Princess Margaret and her husband on a visit to Torquay. The train is composed of a normal two coach set of compartment stock, two corridor coaches and then the Special Saloon W9002 (now preserved at Didcot), plus BFK W7372 in the rear. Beside No.5153 is the shunting neck for the carriage sidings, now occupied by the terminus of the Torbay Steam Railway. [J. R. Besley]

With Class A headlamps up, No.4574 draws out of Paignton goods yard in June 1962 with two of the Newton Abbot breakdown vans after its gang had re-railed a wagon – by jacking, packing and slewing – in one of the sidings. The Paignton-Goodrington area was the operating focal point along this line and the layout was improved here under the governments 'relief of unemployment' programme in the early 1930s, including a new goods shed and sidings. On the latter on peak Saturdays, all wagons were cleared away so that every possible foot of space could be used for passenger stock.

[J. R. Besley]

Unusual duty for a 'King' – No.6018 *King Henry VI* propelling empty stock out of the carriage sidings into Paignton station for an up working, 21 July 1962. No.6018 ran back light engine to Goodrington to take over a Paddington train later in the day. Considerable restrictions existed on the working of the 60xx class anywhere off the main running lines, most sidings and goods loops being barred to them except in emergency.

[J. R. Besley]

No.6965 *Thirlestaine Hall* with a train of empty SR stock for Kingswear in connection with a River Dart excursion, waits for the electric token alongside Goodrington signal box on 11 May 1962. Behind the train the down loop is being used to stable a rake of passenger stock. Considerable development of the layout at Goodrington took place from 1928-32; prior to this had been a mere halt, with a loop. [J. R. Besley]

Wind off the sea blows steam down over 0-6-0PT No.9633 heading a train of sixteen coal wagons which it has brought up from Kingswear, 21 March 1961. Below, another loaded coal train behind No.5154 passing Goodrington on 3 September 1962 bound for Torquay gasworks. The fan of four carriage sidings on the right were laid in the mid-1950s at the same time that other improvements were introduced here – including the replacement of the level-crossing by an overbridge – to increase operational efficiency. [J. R. Besley]

The 12.45 branch goods from Paignton yard to Kingswear on 21 March 1961 passing Waterside Camp. On this occasion it was more of a parcels train, being composed of an ex-GWR toplight brake, a 'Siphon G', a BR GUV, plus a 'Toad'. The sun shines brightly on Torbay, and Torquay can be seen across the water, but it is cold enough for the exhaust from No.9633 to show up well. [J. R. Besley]

A vacuum operated 55' turntable was included in the additional facilities provided at Goodrington in the mid-1950s to help cope with locomotive servicing, as hitherto they had always had to work back to Newton Abbot for this. A watertank and mess rooms for the crews were provided but no coaling facilities. 2-6-0 No.6372, 'spotted' on the turntable on 6 July 1961, has the inscription 'Royal Engine' chalked on the smokebox – a reference to its use about this date to haul the Royal Train some way up the Ashburton branch for an overnight stay.
[J. R. Besley]

No.1001 *County of Bucks* – borrowed by Newton Abbot shed from Penzance – heads the 1.50 p.m. Kingswear to Paddington through Goodrington Sands Halt on 30 March 1961. As it is Easter weekend, this is being run as a separate through train, whereas normally it is usually two or three coaches only and added to the up 'Royal Duchy'. The train is just leaving the single-line section and running down grade. Note the crossover is broken by a catch-point to stop any runaway should it over-run the home signal.
Thus a train at the up platform would be protected.
[J. R. Besley]

The graceful Hookhills Viaduct crosses the small valley where the road runs down to Broadsands beach and this name is locally better known for the viaduct than the official one of Hookhills. No.5992 *Horton Hall* heads the 4.10 p.m. Kingswear-Taunton across its nine spans on 4 October 1962. This was the last regular steam duty on the line.

[J. R. Besley]

Immaculate in fresh green livery and hauling equally clean chocolate-and-cream liveried coaches, 'Castle' No.7000 *Viscount Portal* starts the up Torbay Express' away from Churston on 2 September 1957. This is the junction for the two mile-long Brixham branch which can be seen curving away to the right through the smaller arch of the bridge. In fact the 14xx usual on the branch trains can just be seen taking water beyond No.7000's smokebox. Note the down line is signalled for reversible working to enable passenger trains to call at the principal platform which has much easier access for road vehicles etc. On the left is the line used for stabling fish vans for the Brixham traffic.   [A. R. Butcher]

The northern end of Greenway Tunnel with a 51xx 2-6-2T heading an up local from Kingswear on 2 September 1957. 495 yards long, this bore was a difficult and costly one to drive, being in very hard limestone which required blasting every inch of the way. Much of the stone removed was built into the ten spans of Maypool Viaduct near the southern end. The tunnel is nominally on a 1 in 100 gradient, with a mile and a half leading up to it at 1 in 66, and with 1 in 75 for a distance above this northern portal. A 51xx was allowed 320 tons as maximum load on the run. [A. R. Butcher]

From the passing loop at Churston it is single track to Kingswear, three miles or so of downhill running through Greenway Tunnel on a gradient principally at 1 in 66. Much of this is restricted to 30 mph limit and a permanent speed restriction sign facing up trains can be seen here. No.7924 *Thornycroft Hall* is nearing the end of her journey with the 9.0 a.m. from Wolverhampton in June 1961 – in fact the Kingswear portion of the 'Cornishman' lengthened to run as a full train throughout. At this location on the extremely scenic Kingswear branch, the line formerly ran straight ahead to cross Noss creek on a timber viaduct; in the early 1920s the roadbed was re-routed on a curved embankment around this side inlet of the main Dart estuary.

[W. L. Underhay]

'Castle' Class No.7001 *Sir James Milne* at Kingswear on 2 October 1958 about to depart with the 'Torbay Express'. Leaving at 11.25 a.m., it will arrive in Paddington at 3.35 p.m. taking 4 hours 10 minutes. The roof of the landing stage for the GWR ferry across the estuary to Dartmouth can be seen to the left of the coaster *Speciality*. Coal is being landed from this into wagons to be worked up to the gas works at Torquay.

[J. R. Besley]

A hard push for the crew of No.7316 on the turntable at Kingswear, a terminus where space was rather at a premium for the railway facilities. A curved island platform served the passenger traffic, parallel to the quay where coal was landed from coastal shipping and where the GWR-owned ferry crossed the estuary to Totnes. 'Kings' were allowed to use the branch and were occasionally to be seen on the turntable here. This was installed in 1915, together with additional sidings. The main development of the layout at Kingswear was in 1928-29.

[N. E. Preedy collection]

A general view of Kingswear in April 1961, with 57xx 0-6-0PT No.3796 shunting on the left whilst a column of steam on the right comes from No.5024 *Carew Castle* on the turntable. In the foreground is the 'Torbay Express' with D826 *Jupiter* at the head.   [H. H. Bleads]

28xx class 2-8-0s appeared at Kingswear on coal trains from time to time in the 1950s. No.2805, photographed on 2 October 1958, still has the inside steam pipes of the earlier ones in the class. Maximum load for freights on the branch was 40 wagons but in practice loads were less (usually 30) and banking up to Churston was not infrequent.   [J. R. Besley]

A scene back on the main line two miles or so west of Aller Junction, where a belt conveyor bridges the tracks at Stoneycombe quarries to connect excavations on each side of the line. The gradient here is tightening up towards 1 in 38 and the reverse curves through the woods; No.5058 *Earl of Clancarty* is sweeping downhill with the brakes on leading the 2.10 p.m. from Plymouth to Cardiff on Sunday 16 April 1961. The quarry siding on the left serves the big storage hoppers which supply ballast wagons, stone from here being despatched far and wide for p.w. use.

[W. L. Underhay]

2-6-2T No.5545 on Dainton, running light, April 1961. At this date she had just been transferred down from Machynlleth shed and was due to go to Penzance for some eighteen months before dieselisation moved her on up-country again prior to final withdrawal in 1964. .
[W. L. Underhay]

No.2828, banked by a 51xx 2-6-2T, on the final stretch of the climb up to the 'gabletop' of Dainton, 26 August 1957. The single Aller banker was on duty round the clock every weekday and for more than twelve hours each day at weekends, being supplemented at times by an additional engine from Newton Abbot.
[A. R. Butcher]

No.5040 *Stokesay Castle* with the up 'Royal Duchy' in August 1957, comes over the discernible 'ridge' of Dainton by the tunnel, to commence the run down to Aller Junction. This is the eastern portal and loose-coupled freights stopped here for the guard to pin down brakes, the fireman telephoning back to the signal box at the other end of the tunnel when the train was ready to proceed. The telephone box and bell are just visible on the right. The pinned-down brakes will be lifted at Aller Junction at the foot of the bank.   [A. R. Butcher]

The 61xx 'Prairies' originally belonged to the London area but in the early 1960s they were dispersed to other parts of the Region. No.6113 on 21 May 1963 has a turn of duty with the Taunton District Engineers inspection saloon, and is seen making a swift climb of Dainton after recently relaying with f.b. rail. The white objects between the tracks are alignment posts dumped ready for installation; they give guidance to p.w. gangs in subsequent track maintenance.

[D. M. Cox]

Crossing at Dainton summit, 22 March 1961; No.4908 *Broome Hall* has charge of a Penzance and Plymouth-Manchester express whilst No.4708 is heading west with the 10.40 a.m. Class D freight from Hackney yard. Banking in the rear, in the smoke filled depths of the tunnel is diesel-hydraulic D6307. The stop board in front of No.4708 does not apply as the freight is a partly fitted one. The line to the left is the up refuge siding, 27 wagons long, used by up bankers on occasion; on the right are the down refuge sidings behind the signal box. There were also quarry sidings here in pre-Nationalisation days.

[J. R. Besley]

Leaking a little steam but nevertheless going well even after the adverse and gruelling five miles of climb from Totnes, No.5021 *Whittington Castle* approaches the final 1 in 37 to the summit of Dainton with the 'Cornishman', 26 August 1957. Unassisted a 'Castle' was allowed 350 tons as the standard load eastbound over the South Devon banks, whilst 'Kings' were allowed one bogie more (eleven) than this represented. Note the alignment posts in the 'six foot' and the perfect sweep of the well maintained permanent way.

[A. R. Butcher]

Another view of Dainton summit, by the 218 mp, with No.5028 *Llantillo Castle* working hard on the 7.30 a.m. Penzance-Manchester, in August 1957.

[A. R. Butcher]

No.2846 dropping cautiously down from Dainton summit towards Totnes with a freight for Tavistock in September 1957. Below, No.5076 *Gladiator* with an up milk train from Cornwall at the same location, April 1961.

[A. R. Butcher-
W. L. Underhay]

A Class E freight for Tavistock Junction yard headed by double-chimneyed 'Castle' No.5071 *Spitfire* runs into Totnes on 28 September 1962 and will stop on the down main just beyond the A38 overbridge ready for the banker. This will be a D63xx diesel-hydraulic but in former days was a standard 51xx 2-6-2T duty. From Totnes the climb is initially at 1 in 66 and 1 in 71, followed by stretches at 1 in 47-56-52 up to Tigley signal box three miles away. The banker will come off at Rattery box two more miles further on, where the gradients have eased to a more lenient 1 in 65-90.

[J. R. Besley]

The Plymouth and District Engineers train on a visit to Totnes up platform, 23 October 1952, with 2-6-2T No.4403. This venerable carriage is now preserved on the Dart Valley Railway. Below, activity in the pouring rain at Totnes, 3 October 1958: 0-4-2T No.1470 has arrived off the Ashburton branch with the daily goods, and duty banker No.8 – No.4178 – helps with the task of disposing of her train into the down sidings. No.4145, carrying the bankers duty board No.3, is waiting alongside the up platform.　　　　　　　　　　　　　　　　　　　[J. R. Besley]

An Ocean Liner special
coming down Hemerdon
bank towards Plymouth in
July 1951, headed by
'Star' No.4054 *Princess
Charlotte* and an
unidentified 'Castle'.
Down trains were of
course not run with the
same ultra-fast timing as
those up to Paddington.

[Derek Cross]

Doubleheading was the usual order of the day for up trains out of North Road, ready for the banks between there and Newton Abbot. Here No. 6875 *Hindford Grange* and No. 6008 *King James II* put up an impressive display as they move off with the 'Cornish Riviera' on 31 May 1958. They have a booked 48 minutes for the hard run to Newton Abbot and two minutes there to detach the 'Grange'. Note the dumpy advance starter by the signal box on the right, which disappeared in the power signalling reorganisation at Plymouth a year or two later. A Southern 02 Class 0-4-4--T is visible by the platform, with a Saltash auto-train beyond.

[B. W. Mennie]

North Road station at Plymouth, with No. 1006 *County of Cornwall* after arrival with 'The Royal Duchy' on 19 September 1960. She is about to be detached, one headlamp having already been removed, and another engine is waiting to take the train on to Paddington. At this date No. 1006 was allocated to St. Blazey (83E) and also served for some years at Penzance – although this local 'posting' for one of the 'Counties' was probably only co-incidental. Seen here is North Road station rebuilt in 1908; it replaced Millbay as the main station in the 1920s and the other principal station, Friary, was closed in 1958. A lengthy rebuilding, interrupted by the war and by enemy action during those years, was completed in 1962.

[W. L. Underhay]

0-6-0PT No.6430 on duty as station pilot at North Road on 28 September 1962. With a number of trains terminating here, plus others being divided for Cornwall or with portions from there to be added to up expresses, a considerable amount of work was involved in this. The e.c.s. sidings lay out at Laira, close by the locomotive depot. No.6430, auto-fitted, is now on the Dart Valley Railway. [J. R. Besley]

Beyond Millbay station in Plymouth a network of goods-only lines served Millbay docks with its various commercial wharves and several six-coupled 'humpties' were kept for use over these. No.1361 was one of three or four of the class based on Laira shed which shared dock shunting duty here for many years, post-war. She is seen during lunchbreak at West Wharf on 19 September 1957, complete with the usual shunters truck. These saddletanks were the only types permitted to work the docks sidings here, plus – under exceptional wartime conditions, the 19xx class panniers with their front side rods removed. 'Castles' and the smaller 4-6-0s were allowed to the docks for the 'Ocean Liner' and mail specials. [J. R. Besley]

No.6420 on a two-coach auto train for Saltash on 5 August 1956 photographed on the outskirts of Plymouth where the Southern route to Okehampton and Exeter diverges in the foreground. There was formerly an intensive suburban service in Plymouth, from Saltash through to North Road (or to Millbay until the station there was damaged in an air raid in 1940) with something like forty trains in each direction every weekday. An interesting account of the Plymouth suburban services appears in *Centenary of the Cornwall Railway* by R. J. Woodfin. [T. E. Williams]

An unusual view, taken through the windscreen in the driving cab of a dmu, at the west end of the Royal Albert Bridge at Saltash, No.5098 *Clifford Castle* is coming off the single line over the last of the approach spans and when the section is clear the dmu will be able to proceed. Although *Clifford Castle* is clearing the 15 mph limit, a continuing speed restriction to 35 mph exists for another mile or more through Saltash station, over the sharply curved viaduct and past former 'Defiance' platform. On the right can be seen one of the bridge towers and prominent in the centre is the new single span A38 road bridge under construction. [W. L. Underhay]

The branch down to the coast at Looe diverges at Liskeard – and diverge is truly the word, for it leaves the main line in a sharp curve at right angles and drops very steeply indeed (1 in 34) to the valley running below in the seaward direction. No.5523, on 23 May 1959, waits to depart from the branch platform at Liskeard with the 11.55 a.m. Tenuously the branch survives today.

[M. Mensing]

An up freight behind Mogul No.5350 on the sharp 1 in 59 pull up into Liskeard station from Moorswater Viaduct, 14 June 1956. The gradient profile of the main line west of Plymouth has an irregular saw-tooth pattern, abounding in short variable uphill sections up to 1 in 60 or 80 in severity, and this is combined with a never ending succession of curves. An overall speed limit of 60 mph applies and there is nowhere on the 79 miles between North Road and Penzance that allows much recovery time to a late running train.

[M. Mensing]

W 5666 W

Another 45xx, No.4552, on a Looe-Liskeard train approaching Sandplace Halt on 6 June 1961. Most of the branch follows the former route of a canal.

[L. Elsey]

Not much more than a touch of the regulator will be needed to get 'Castle' Class No.5092 *Tresco Abbey* away from the stop at Bodmin Road for the gradient drops away sharply from the station here at 1 in 65 towards Lostwithiel. The train is from Manchester, on 18 May 1959. Some idea of the sinous nature of the Cornwall main line can be seen from the reverse curves visible here beyond the goods shed. [M. Mensing]

Coaled up, watered and with her safety valves blowing off, No.6397 is obviously ready for duty alongside the coal stage at St. Blazey shed, 10 July 1955. This depot served the clay lines of mid-Cornwall including the two which ran through to Fowey, the main port of shipment. It also provided motive power for the long and heavily graded Newquay branch over which No.6397 was a regular, both on local services and also acting as pilot to the train engines of through expresses to the resort. At one period shortly after the Second World War one could see twelve-coach trains on the branch doubleheaded by a 'Castle' and a 'Bulldog', with a banking engine in rear to help up the stiff climb to Luxulyan. [R. S. Carpenter]

Pannier tanks of one class or another were the mainstay of the many china clay branches around St. Austell and St. Blazey, able to work in and out of the numerous privately-owned sidings of the clay 'dries'. The 45xx Prairies would have been ideal but were prohibited from many of these and a considerable amount of doubleheading by panniers was needed on branches such as Carbean, Retew, and elsewhere, where 1 in 40 was the ruling gradient. Here No.9755 heads along the floor of the Luxulyan valley near St. Blazey with a rake of clay empties on 3 August 1956. [L. Elsey]

Another of the St. Blazey panniers, but on the main line between there and Lostwithiel, with No.8702 on a short p.w. work train, 13 June 1956. The setting is the east end of Treverrin Tunnel, with the tiny box of that name visible by the up line beyond the train. In the foreground a colourlight signal is almost ready for installation which will replace the semaphore and also enable Treverrin signal box to be dispensed with. It had served to provide an intermediate section between the continuously manned boxes at Lostwithiel and Par, being open during the day and useful at busy times to help the traffic flow over the Treverrin climb. This was a 'hump', with two mile long gradients at up to 1 in 62 or so in each direction, and was used by the clay trains routed from St. Blazey to Fowey via Lostwithiel.

[M. Mensing]

No. 7823 *Hook Norton Manor,* of Truro shed, running light on the up line towards St. Austell station. A minor feature of this section and along other stretches of the main line in Cornwall is the profusion still surviving today of massive rhododendrons growing wild or semi-wild along the sides of the railway. Near Menheniot one can even see the tall white-flowering tree-heather growing in some of the cuttings.
[P. Q. Treloar

Truro was the main centre west of Plymouth for passenger traffic, with three main platforms plus the Falmouth bay Here No.6300 has just backed on to the Falmouth portion from the 9.30 a.m. Paddington to Penzance, 18 September 1957. On the up line, a p.w. gang are using a track gauge under the eye of the foreman ganger.
[P. Q. Treloar]

No.1002 *County of Berks* leaving Highertown Tunnel at the west end of Truro station with 'The 'Royal Duchy' on a September morning in 1957.   [P. Q. Treloar]

Another scene in the Highertown cutting, with 2-6-2T No.4554 departing with a freight for the Falmouth branch in the early 1950s. Beyond lies the running shed and the rural outskirts of this Cornish city. Note the narrow arms of the vintage signal in the foreground.   [P. Q. Treloar]

Mogul No.7333, in lined green livery, tackles the 1 in 60 away from Truro after a lengthy stop with the mid-morning parcels, run overnight from Paddington. This conveyed also sundry e.c.s. and the occasional milk tank wagon left over from the principal trains of empties worked down by night to the West Country.
[P. Q. Treloar]

Displaying the rather angular utilitarian lines typical of the 'Counties', No. 1007 *County of Brecknock* storms away from Truro with a fitted freight for Marazion. She has run through Truro without a stop and the regulator is being opened up again to the full to cope with the bank ahead after the regulation slowing to 30 mph through the station.

[P. Q. Treloar]

The long public footbridge spanning the goods yard and the down end of the platforms at Truro was a well-known vantage point for enthusiasts. This scene, photographed from there, is of No.4574 coming into the yard with a short freight from Carn Brea, on 21 September 1959. Truro West box, seen beyond the brake van, controlled movements around the shed, the west end of the station and the main line out to Penwethers Junction where the Falmouth and Newham branches diverged from it at the far end of Highertown Tunnel.

[P. Q. Treloar]

No.8485 on duty as station pilot at Truro takes on a full brake out from the down platform after it has been left by an earlier westbound parcels train and will set it back into the bay on the right for subsequent attachment to a Falmouth local. The Newquay services also started and terminated here, making Truro a busy centre in steam days in summer for both local and long distance trains.

[P. Q. Treloar]

Before road hauliers secured the major part of the traffic in agricultural produce from West Cornwall, there was a continuing flow of filled freights bound to or from Marazion and Ponsandane siding outside Penzance. No.5020 *Tremarton Castle* – named after one of Cornwall's castles but not a local engine, being from Cardiff (Canton) – waits for the road westward in Truro goods loop with empty vans on 22 May 1959. Normally this would be a turn for a 'Hall' or a 'Grange' but with diesel-hydraulics starting to come into service a few 'Castles' were spare from their normal top link duties.

[P. Q. Treloar]

The 'Counties' were quite well thought of by enginemen in Cornwall and did good work there, particularly on 'The Cornishman'. Truro shed's No.1023 *County of Oxford* is being cleaned ready for the 4.15 p.m. 'school train' to Penzance – a local fill-in working which enabled it to be booked thereafter for the 8.45 p.m. sleeper to Paddington. In the foreground No.4588 is now visible, now owned by the Dart Valley Railway and rescued from Barry scrapyard after withdrawal from BR service.

[P. Q. Treloar]

No.5098 *Clifford Castle* with an evening Plymouth-Penzance semi-fast heads round the curves towards Chacewater in July 1961 near the top of the three miles at 1 in 80 west of Truro. By coincidence this is the longest evenly graded stretch of line anywhere west of Dawlish, for short rapidly varying gradients are the order of the day; in the next six miles from this location, for example, there are no less than 27 gradient posts marking the changes.

[M. J. Messenger]

No.6913 *Levens Hall,* a mile or so west of the previous location, is over the crest of the climb from Truro and is heading west for Chacewater and the next stop at Redruth. The sharp curves seen here, leading to Chacewater viaduct, show how essential the permanent overall 60 mph speed limit was necessary in Cornwall. Point-to-point running lines were strictly adhered to when expresses were running late, due to the nature of the road. [M. Mensing]

The leisurely 3.35 p.m. all stations from Penzance -Truro coasts into Chacewater station on 20 May 1959 behind No.6805 *Broughton Grange*. On the right are the lines serving the Perranporth and Newquay branch which diverges just west of here. At an elevation here of several hundred feet, compared to near sea-level at Truro, the line is up on the spine of the county and sea mists drifting in from the Atlantic are frequent in summer, as on this occasion.

[M. Mensing]

The hard two-cylinder exhaust of No.1007 *County of Brecknock* echoes over Gwinear Road on 19 September 1959 as her driver gets a Penzance-Crewe perishables train rapidly under way from the station. In the Helston Bay, No.4588 is resting between shunting moves.　　　　　　　　　　　　　　　　　　　　　　　　　　　　　　[P. Q. Treloar]

A typical scene at Helston, terminus of the single line branch running south from Gwinear Road on the main line: No.4540 with an afternoon train is just starting the nine-mile run back through Nancegollan to the main line. The entire branch was closed in the 1960s and together with Gwinear Road, is now just a memory.　　[P. Q. Treloar]

One might venture an opinion that nowhere else on the GWR was more expected of the 'Halls' and their crews than in Cornwall, where they regularly worked twelve-coach trains without fuss or comment despite the numerous banks steeper than 1 in 70. Stamina and not speed was called for, needing a free-steaming boiler and decent coal . . . . Here, No.4908 *Broome Hall* is crossing Angarrack Viaduct near Hayle and is on a one mile section of adverse 1 in 61 on a Saturday in July 1958, with the eleven coaches of the 10.20 a.m. Penzance to Swansea – within the 380 ton standard load limit allowed in GWR days for the class. It is interesting to note that 'Granges' were officially allowed five tons more – 385 tons.

[P. Q. Treloar]

The private wharves served by the Hayle branch were horse-worked, as seen here in July 1959, on the siding alongside the A30 main road. Crossing the viaduct carrying the main line is 2-6-2T No.4571 heading back to Ponsandane goods yard after shunting at Hayle.

[P. Q. Treloar]

A broccoli special from Marazion, also near Angarrack, heading east behind No.6845 *Paviland Grange*. In spring a considerable number of these trains were run conveying early vegetables to markets up-country. In 1945 for example over 660 specials were run from West Cornwall, conveying either new potatoes or broccoli. Latterly large numbers of redundant XP cattle wagons were allocated for use on these trains.

[P. Q. Treloar]

St. Ives has changed somewhat in the quarter century since this photograph was taken in August 1950; the 'Cornish Riviera' is departing for St. Erth, headed by two 45xx tanks, and will go on from there as a separate portion, hauled probably by a 'Castle'. The sixth carriage is a GWR Kitchen car. The three-coach branch set in the foreground is still lettered GWR and bears destination boards.   [B. A. Butt]

No.4566, now on the Severn Valley Railway, draws away from Lelant station on the St. Ives branch, 14 April 1960.   Below, No.6824 *Ashley Grange* has brought additional vehicles out of the United Dairies Creamery sidings at St. Erth and backs down to add them to the existing load from Penzance which were left standing by the up platform. No shunter existed here and main line engines marshalled their own trains, as was also the case at Lostwithiel. Even 'Castles' were permitted to use the creamery sidings for this purpose.   [P. Q. Treloar]

'County' Class No.1023 *County of Oxford* with the down 'Cornish Riviera' express in July 1954 leaving St. Erth, seen in original condition, with single chimney, in contrast to the later style as seen on page 82. A well-known West Country 'County', she was allocated to Truro when new in 1947 and apart from a spell at Laira served there for many years. Stabled on the line in the foreground are 'empty diners', a train of these dining cars and restaurant cars being worked down the west on Fridays ready for the rush of holiday expresses and relief run on summer Saturdays.

[P. Q. Treloar]

No.6988 *Swithland Hall* passing Marazion station with the down milk and parcels for Penzance, 11 May 1959. Bringing up the rear is a gas tank wagon, whilst the rest of the load is doubtless more or less empty stock being returned to Penzance for subsequent loading. Milk in churns, from Newbridge creamery west of Penzance was formerly loaded in the sidings adjoining the terminus, together with milk in bulk from road tankers. In addition the parcels vans may be for use in connection with flowers or other traffic from the Isles of Scilly.   [M. Mensing]

Barely a revenue-earning load for No.4083 *Abbotsbury Castle,* photographed on the main line alongside Long Rock locomotive depot with an up broccoli special. More wagons are probably due to be added at St. Erth and perhaps Gwinear Road. On the right a 'County' is backing down to the shed out of sight behind No.4083.

[P. Q. Treloar]

There was plenty of work to be done shunting empty coaching stock at Penzance, for the confined layout of the terminus and the cramped portion of the running lines right alongside the shore hemmed in by the road meant that some coaches had to be taken out as far as the sidings east of Marazion, to be stabled. In the holiday season, in addition to sleeping cars, the 'postal', and some stock for perishable traffic, room had to be found for a very considerable number of coaches for the Saturday peaks. These two scenes in the summer of 1950 show No.9717 (above) bringing twelve coaches of very mixed vintage towards Marazion and No.8409, nearer Penzance, similarly engaged. The shunters' 'gig' is, as always, in evidence – the one from Penzance Goods having also been pressed into use above to supplement the normal Penzance Passenger.

[B. A. Butt]

Penzance station was originally the terminus of the West Cornwall Railway – a wooden structure in typical Brunel style housing a solitary platform and not unlike a slightly enlarged version of Moretonhampstead station as seen on page 9. In 1921 additional siding accommodation was provided on the seaward side, by reclaiming ground below the existing highwater mark, whilst in the mid-1930s the station itself was rebuilt and the platforms extended. In this scene in July 1959 a 'Castle' is waiting to depart with the 8.55 a.m. to Plymouth, whilst a recently arrived express and a later departure occupy the two centre platforms.

[P. H. Hanson]

NOR
AIRPOWER

NORDIC AIRPOWER

Jan Jørgensen

Airlife
England

ACKNOWLEDGEMENTS

The photographs in *Nordic Airpower* were taken during numerous visits to several Nordic air bases over the last five years. The author would like to express his sincere thanks to all officers and air crews for their generous hospitality and support during these visits, and naturally also for providing the photographic facilities required for producing this book.

Even though the author has travelled extensively across the landscapes of the varied and beautiful North and fallen in love with the friendly people of the Nordic countries, it has been impossible to photograph all aspects of Nordic military aviation personally. Therefore, a number of friends have assisted him with photographic material for *Nordic Airpower*, and his thanks goes to the following for both large and small contributions: Scott van Aken, Peter Foster, Steen Hartov, Christoph Kugler, Jyrki Laukkanen, Peter Liander, Per Nielsen, Anders Nýlen and Thorbjörn Olsen.

Copyright © 1993 by Jan Jørgensen

First published in the UK in 1993
by Airlife Publishing Ltd.

British Library Cataloguing in Publication Data
A catalogue record for this book is
available from the British Library.

ISBN 1 85310 415 9

Printed in Singapore by Kyodo Printing PTE Ltd.

Airlife Publishing Ltd

101 Longden Road, Shrewsbury SY3 9EB

FOREWORD

NORDIC AIRPOWER covers contemporary military aviation activities within the five north European nations of Denmark, Finland, Iceland, Norway and Sweden. Traditionally the Nordic countries regard themselves as members of the same family, even though their historical and political backgrounds are fundamentally very different. Denmark, Iceland and Norway today constitute NATO's northern flank while Finland and Sweden still remain neutral. These diversities have among other things resulted in very interesting and differently equipped Nordic air forces.

COVER CAPTIONS

(Front page top)

JAS39 Gripen lightweight multi-role fighter prototype No.2 was flown for the first time at 19:49 local time on 4 May 1990, with SAAB test pilot Arne Lindholm at the controls. So far *Flygvapnet* has ordered 140 Gripens for delivery during the 1993-2001 period, which are sufficient for re-equipping eight *Divisioner* (Squadrons), but follow-on orders are expected as *Flyvapnet* long-term planning involves a total of 16 SAAB Gripen *Divisioner*, the type eventually replacing both the SAAB Draken and Viggen. (*SAAB*)

(Front page bottom left)

With Swedish type designation HKP9A this MBB BO.105CB operated by *Arméflygbataljon 1* at Boden is demonstrating NoE flying (Nap of Earth) during a visit to Malmsätt. This highly potent anti-tank helicopter is armed with the SAAB/Emerson HeliTOW guidance and control system which allows very accurate use of AGM-71 TOW anti-armour missiles. (*Author*)

(Front page bottom right)

F-16B ET-614 of *Eskadrille 723* inbound for Ålborg at 32,000ft after a visit to RAF Coltishall. Danish Falcons often visit the UK and routinely take part in air defence exercises such as 'Mallet Blow' and 'Elder Joust'. (*Per Nielsen*)

(Rear page top left)

Lockheed C-130H Hercules 954 of *Skvadron 335* from Gardermoen performing an impressive Jet Assisted Take-Off (JATO) during an airshow at Bardufoss. (*Author*)

(Rear page top right)

Piper Arrow IV PA-11 banking high in the sky is operated by the *Koelentokeskus* (Flight Test Centre) at Halli AB. Four of these light aircraft are used by different *Ilmavoimat* units for local liaison duties. (*Jyrki Laukkanen*)

(Rear page bottom)

Attractive air-to-air study of *Ilmavoimat* MiG-21F MG-77 banking above massive clouds. This older Fishbed-C version remained in service with the *Tiedustelulentolaivue* (Reconnaissance Squadron) at Tikkakoski AB until January 1986, equipped with special recce-pods produced by VALMET. Powered by a 12,700lb Tumansky R-11F-300 afterburning turbojet, the MiG-21F was capable of Mach 2.0 at altitude and had a thrust-to-weight ratio of about 0.65. It was generally considered a fine daylight interceptor with excellent handling qualities but the lack of all-weather instrumentation seriously restricted its operational usefulness, especially in a climatical scenario such as that of Finland. (*Jyrki Laukkanen*)

ROYAL DANISH AIR FORCE

Like many other NATO air arms, the *Kongelige Danske Flyvevåben* (Royal Danish Air Force) today employs the General Dynamics F-16 Fighting Falcon as its fighter backbone, with four *Eskadriller* (squadrons) operating this versatile combat aircraft. For many years the primary *Flyvevåbnet* (air force) role within NATO strategy was to maintain an effective control over the shallow Danish straits, which the former Soviet Baltic Fleet had to pass in order to reach open water in the North Sea and Atlantic Ocean.

After the disintegration of the Warsaw Pact the military threat against Denmark and NATO has changed considerably, and *Flyvevåbnet* has quickly adapted to newly-developed NATO tactics by placing a joint Danish-Norwegian F-16 squadron at the disposal of NATO's new Rapid Reaction Force. This assignment is possible because *Flyvevåbnet* already has implemented very flexible operational concepts for its F-16 force, routinely practising multi-role missions (all *Eskadriller* qualified for both air defence and surface attack), air-refuelling (from USAF KC-135 tankers) and dispersed operations (deployments including civil airfields).

Because Greenland and the Faroe Islands are Danish territory *Flyvevåbnet* also has commitments in the North Atlantic area. These mainly comprise SAR duty, fishery inspection and local liaison, which is provided by one Gulfstream III permanently based at Søndre Strømfjord on the Greenland west coast and Westland Lynx helicopters of the *Søværnets Flyvetjeneste* (Naval Air Service) onboard Danish Navy inspection vessels. The Danish Army also controls an independent aviation component, with Fennec anti-tank and Hughes 500 utility helicopters operated by the *Hærens Flyvetjeneste* (Army Air Corps).

Presently *Flyvevåbnet* is suffering a comprehensive reduction and restructuring process, which most importantly has resulted in the retirement of two *Eskadriller* equipped with SAAB Draken fighter-bombers.

Below: Falcon E-195 of *Eskadrille 723* lands at its home base of Ålborg. Danish F-16s often carry orange high-visibility AIM-9 Sidewinder training rounds on their wingtip stations for easy identification of friend/foe during Air Combat Manoeuvring. (*Author*)

Below: All Danish Falcon squadrons have a couple of
F-16B operational trainers at their disposal, like this
Eskadrille 726 example about to touch-down at
Ålborg AB. When the SAAB RF-35 Draken is
withdrawn from use *Eskadrille 726* is expected to take
over the recce-role with a special photo/IRLS recce-
pod presently being developed for the F-16 by
Flyvevåbnet. (*Author*)

Opposite: The pilot of a *Flyvevåbnet* F-16A Fighting
Falcon waits for taxi clearance before take-off, having
completed pre-flight tests and with the 25,000lb static
thrust F100-PW-200 afterburning turbofan running
idle. (*Author*)

Below: Flight-line shot in the *Eskadrille 726* squadron area at Ålborg. During normal peacetime operations *Flyvevåbnet* combat aircraft are turned around on flight-lines with built-in fuel stations and maintenance kits, but are parked in hardened aircraft shelters (HAS) during the night. (*Author*)

Opposite: F-16A E-604 of *Eskadrille 723* flies above the clouds with 1400-litre drop tanks on the inner underwing stations and ejector for a pair of M-55 training bomblets (which simulate 500lb Mk82 low-drag bombs) on the outer underwing stations. All *Flyvevåbnet* Falcon squadrons are multi-role tasked and fully operational in both air defence and surface attack missions, including missiles such as AIM-9L/N Sidewinder and AGM-65F Maverick and standard free-fall bombs in their weaponry. (*Per Nielsen*)

Below: E-604 of *Eskadrille 723* at Ålborg on a local
sortie. From 1995 the entire *Flyvevåbnet* Falcon fleet
will go through a Mid-Life Update programme,
including among other things an improved
Westinghouse AN/APG-66(V) fire control radar as
well as preparations for NVG equipment (Night Vision
Goggles) and FLIR pod (Forward-Looking Infra-Red).
This will enable the F-16A/B to utilise next-generation
air-to-air and air-to-surface weapons systems and
enhance low-level operations under poor weather
conditions and at night. MLU will make Danish F-16s
serviceable until at least year 2010. (*Per Nielsen*)

Opposite: F-16B ET-614 of *Eskadrille 723* inbound for
Ålborg at 32,000ft after a visit to RAF Coltishall. Danish
Falcons often visit Great Britain and routinely take part
in UK air defence exercises such as 'Mallet Blow' and
'Elder Joust'. (*Per Nielsen*)

Below: Karup-based F-35 A-018 of *Eskadrille 725* in an almost vertical climb in full afterburner. Not a particularly typical manoeuvre for the 'mud-moving' Draken fighter-bomber, but a very nice pose for the benefit of the photographer. (*Steen Hartov*)

Opposite: A pair of *Eskadrille 725* F-35 Drakens are seen making training landings at Karup. The student pilot flying A-004 is accompanied by an experienced pilot in A-002, who performs an overshoot while the other Draken touches down. With its distinctive double-delta wing configuration and unique bumper tail-wheel, the Draken has often confused local NATO air traffic controllers when an *Eskadrille 725* or *729* pilot on finals radios 'Four greens — no flaps', confirming that he is approaching in landing configuration! (*Author*)

Below: A head-on view of an F-35 sitting on its *Eskadrille 725* dispersal at Karup AB, clearly showing the nose-mounted laser range-finder which was introduced during 1982-86 with the Weapons Delivery & Navigation System update. This modification programme involved installation of FLIR, HUD, INS and mission computer, giving the older Draken a firing/bombing accuracy equal to — and under visual conditions even better than — the new F-16 Fighting Falcon. (*Author*)

Opposite: A flight of three *Eskadrille 725* Drakens 'down on the deck' fly low over the North Sea off the west coast of Jylland. The Danish F-35 (SAAB designation A35XD) is a special fighter-bomber version of Sweden's J35 air defence fighter, with a strengthened airframe to accommodate heavy ground-attack armament on nine weapons pylons and a 30 per cent increase in fuel capacity. Many electronics were also modified for compatibility with NATO standards, including TACAN, IFF and RWR. (*Steen Hartov*)

Below: RF-35 AR-111 of *Eskadrille 729* in 'clean' configuration without the pair of large 1275-litre under-fuselage drop tanks usually carried by *Flyvevåbnet* Drakens. RF-35 is a recce/fighter version of Draken with five Vinten cameras mounted in the nose section (45-300mm lenses), although the forward-facing camera has now been replaced by a laser range-finder to improve the aircraft's weapons delivery accuracy in the fighter-bomber role. (*Author*)

Opposite: On 18 May 1991 *Eskadrille 725* celebrated its 40-year Jubilee by painting Draken A-009 in a bright red colour scheme with a large yellow dragon on the underside (the squadron insignia). This immaculate F-35 soon became nicknamed *Red Baron* and is seen here flying above massive clouds in formation with TF-35 trainer AT-153. Only seven months later *Eskadrille 725* was disbanded and before the end of 1993 its sister squadron at Karup, *Eskadrille 729*, will also disband and thus the SAAB 35 Draken will disappear from *Flyvevåbnet's* inventory. (*Steen Hartov*)

Below: *Eskadrille 721* Gulfstream III F-330, in a typical operational setting, flying low over vast areas of water on fishery protection duties. With its nose-mounted APS-127 radar the G-III very effectively searches the North Atlantic for trawlers fishing in Danish territorial waters without permission. (*Author*)

Opposite: Three long-range Gulfstream III special mission aircraft are used by *Eskadrille 721* for fishery inspection, sea surveillance, ice reconnaissance, search and rescue, medical evacuation and local transport around Greenland and the Faroe Islands. For this purpose one G-III is deployed to Søndre Strømfjord (Sonderstrom AB) on a rotational basis, but actually *Eskadrille 721* spends more than 85 per cent of its Gulfstream flying hours in the Northern Atlantic and Arctic regions, while sorties to the Faroe Islands usually are flown out of its home base, Værløse. (*Author*)

Top right: Using suitable radio call-sign 'Baby 30' SAAB T-17 Supporter T-430 of the *Flyveskolen* (Flying School) is flying over the green countryside of Southern Sjælland, not far from its home base Avnø. With more than 22,000 air movements annually (mostly touch-and-goes) the small grass field at Avnø has been the centre for Danish military flying training for more than 60 years, but in January 1993 the school moved to Karup and Avnø was closed down. (*Author*)

Below right: SAAB T-17 Supporter T-423 flies low over the *Storstrøm* bridge not far from the small peninsula which houses Avnø AB. Besides serving as basic trainer, this Swedish-built light aircraft is also used for liaison flying, refresher training, spare parts cargo etc, with local Station Flights at all major *Flyvevåbnet* AB. (*Author*)

Opposite: A busy morning scene at the Avnø flight-line during routine T-17 training operations. *Flyveskolen* is mainly tasked with selection of suitable pilot candidates, each receiving 25 hours of basic flying training at Avnø AB with a required solo graduation after only 12 hours. Then follows a one-year flying training course in the United States, where fighter pilot candidates receive 260 hours on USAF T-37B and T-38A with the Euro-NATO Joint Jet Pilot Training Centre at Sheppard AFB in Texas, while transport and helicopter candidates go to various USN Training Wings. (*Author*)

Below: Lockheed C-130H Hercules B-678 of *Eskadrille 721* touches down at its home base of Værløse in a new all-grey paint scheme. Repainting is part of a Danish C-130 Update Programme introduced in 1990, involving improved TACAN/INS, OMEGA navigation system, Digital Autopilot, Flight Data Recorder, AN/ALR-69 Radar Warning Receiver and chaff/flare dispenser. The RWR/dispenser system is especially important when flying on humanitarian relief missions to the many troubled areas of the world, where small but deadly guided/homing SAM missile systems are becoming increasingly commonplace. (*Author*)

Opposite: *Eskadrille 721* at Værløse is using three C-130H Hercules for heavy duty transport all over the world, ranging from UN relief missions in hot and sunny Africa to liaison flights into freezing cold Arctic outposts on Greenland. Normal day-to-day operations involve the scheduled 'Shuttle Train' route between Værløse and the NATO headquarters at Karup. (*Author*)

Below: S-61A U-275 of *Eskadrille 722* at Værløse AB flies over Roskilde Fjord. Following several updates (including improved avionics, weather radar and FLIR) the Sea King is expected to remain in service until the year 2000. (*Author*)

Opposite: After more than 25 years of flying with eight Sikorsky S-61A Sea Kings, *Eskadrille 722* at Værløse has accumulated some 75,000 hours on this large and effective SAR helicopter. With S-61s deployed for continuous SAR readiness at Værløse, Skrydstrup and Ålborg (plus Rønne on the island of Bornholm during winter), *Eskadrille 722* has saved more than 4000 lives. (*Author*)

Below: *Hærens Flyvetjeneste* (Army Air Corps) at
Vandel AB is using the small and extremely
manoeuvrable Hughes 500M for battlefield scouting,
light transport, FAC and Medevac. It is also used in
a civilian role, ferrying police observers on traffic
surveillance duties. (*Author*)

Opposite: A pair of Army H500M in close formation
over a typical central Jylland landscape, not far from
their home base of Vandel. The Hughes 500 is an
observation/liaison helicopter and in Danish service it
has never been armed with any form of weaponry —
other than the crews' personal hand-guns! (*Author*)

Below: Danish Army Fennec P-288 without its TOW weaponry system, hovers in front of a shelter at Vandel AB. According to Danish Army tactics the anti-tank helicopters will be deployed operationally in four platoons, each equipped with three TOW-armed Fennec tank-killers and one H.500M scout helicopter. (*Author*)

Right: On 15 August 1990 the first of 12 AS550C2 Fennec helicopters were delivered to Vandel AB from Aérospatiale in France, thereby for the first time providing the Danish Army with a very potent airborne anti-tank combat element. Fennec was chosen following evaluation of other helicopter types, including the Bell 406CS, Hughes 500MD and MBB BO105. (*Author*)

Below: Aérospatiale AS550C2 Fennec anti-tank helicopter P-352 of *Hærens Flyvetjeneste* flies over the countryside near Vandel AB. This view clearly shows the side-mounted TOW missile launcher pods and roof-mounted HeliTOW guidance/control system originally developed by SAAB Instruments and Emerson Electronics for the Swedish Army BO105CB anti-tank helicopters. (*Author*)

Opposite: Hughes 500M H-203 was the first to be painted in the new black/green Army camouflage introduced with the delivery of Fennec anti-tank helicopters. (*Author*)

Overleaf: *Søværnets Flyvetjeneste* (Naval Air Service) is based at Værløse outside Copenhagen with its eight Lynx helicopters, but is tasked operationally far from home. The unit's major roles include fishery inspection, SAR and local liaison in the icy waters of the North Atlantic around Greenland and the Faroe Islands. When operating in this theatre the Lynx is deployed onboard Danish Navy vessels of the 'Beskytteren' and 'Hvidbjørnen' classes, the latter soon to be replaced by newly-constructed 'Thetis' class vessels. (*Author*)

Below: Lynx S-175 of *Søværnets Flyvetjeneste* (Naval Air Service) flies over Roskilde Fjord, west of its home base at Værløse. Currently the operational capability of the Danish Lynx is being considerably increased by an extensive update programme, comprising installation of an integrated RACAL Tactical Data System and FLIR which will improve OTHT-capacity (Over The Horizon Targeting) of the Lynx, when operating with Navy vessels armed with surface-to-surface missiles. (*Author*)

Right: Westland Lynx Mk80 S-191 poses for the photographer in front of Møns Klint, the Danish equivalent of Britain's white cliffs of Dover. Note the nose-mounted 'Orange Reaper' RWR sensors which have been introduced as part of a recent update programme. (*Author*)

FINNISH AIR FORCE

Today the *Suomen Ilmavoimat* (Finnish Air Force) is primarily a fighter defence force with only limited strike capability. This is a direct consequence of the Paris Peace Treaty signed at the end of World War Two, according to which *Ilmavoimat* strength is limited to 3000 men and 60 combat aircraft armed only with non-offensive weaponry.

Furthermore Finland's security policy has been highly influenced by its great eastern neighbour, the former Soviet Union. After several wars between the two nations, peaceful relations have been guaranteed since 1948 through the Treaty of Friendship, Cooperation and Mutual Assistance. According to the military articles of this Treaty, Finland is to remain armed neutral and achieve peace in agreement with the principles of the United Nations.

Front-line *Ilmavoimat* combat aircraft are operated by three regional *Lennosto* (air defence wings), each equipped with one *Hävittäjälentolaivue* (fighter squadron) of Draken or MiG-21 interceptors, supplemented by BAe Hawk trainers and light communication aircraft. Finland has an indigenous aircraft industry, with Valmet not only producing the L-70 Vinka and L-90 Redigo military trainers but also assembling Drakens and Hawks acquired by the *Ilmavoimat*.

Recently Finland decided to replace its fighter force with the McDonnell Douglas F/A-18 Hornet, the deal comprising seven two-seat F/A-18D to be delivered from the McDonnell Douglas production line in 1995 followed by 57 single-seat F/A-18C assembled locally by Valmet. The Hornet was chosen in preference to the F-16C/D Falcon, Mirage 2000-5, SAAB 39 Gripen and MiG-29 because of best cost effectiveness during a planned 30-year lifetime.

Below: MG-119 taxis for take-off at the start of a long-range navigation training mission from Kuopio-Rissala. This MiG-21bis carries three 490-litre auxiliary fuel tanks on the centreline and outer under-wing stations which provide an increased range of about 50 per cent. Standard air-to-air weaponry includes K-13A missiles (both the IR-homing AA-2 'Atoll' and the radar guided AA-2-2 'Advanced Atoll' versions) as well as the more effective R-60 (AA-8 'Aphid') advanced dogfight missile. (*Author*)

Below: MiG-21bis 'Fishbed-N' MG-117 of *Hävittäjälentolaivue 31* taxies off the runway at Kuopio-Rissala after a local air defence training sortie. The large conical centrebody in the nose can move in/out to give variable air intake geometry, and also contains a pulse search and track radar designated 'Jay Bird' by NATO. Also clearly visible is the black/yellow striped anti-blast plates above the semi-recessed twin-barrel 23mm GSh-23L gun pack fitted under the fuselage. (*Author*)

Opposite: *Ilmavoimat* MiG-21bis MG-131 banks above a snow covered Finnish winter landscape. The MiG-21bis 'Fishbed-N' superseded the older MiG-21F 'Fishbed-C' in Finnish service, and represents a completely new generation of fighter technology with improvements affecting both airframe structure, avionics/weapons systems and powerplant. Installation of the powerful 16,800lb Tumansky R-25-300 engine has raised thrust-to-weight ratio of the MiG-21bis to about 0.95 in normal air-air configuration, increasing to 1.1 if only two AA-2-2 Advanced Atoll missiles and 50 per cent fuel are carried. In this later condition the theoretical climb rate of the bis is not much inferior to that of the F-16A with similar armament and fuel, however the Falcon has double the rate of turn at sea level and only 90 per cent of the MiG's turn radius. (*Jyrki Laukkanen*)

Below and opposite: MiG-21bis MG-140 manoeuvres above clouds, painted in new toned-down markings introduced during the late 1980s. For more than 30 years the airbase at Kuopio-Rissala has been synonymous with MiG operations. Parent unit for *Ilmavoimat* MiGs has always been *Hävittäjälentolaivue 31* (Fighter Squadron 31), organised within the *Karjalan Lennosto* (Karelian Wing) at Kuopio-Rissala, which is responsible for airspace surveillance and command/control of interceptors within south-eastern Finland. (*Jyrki Laukkanen*)

Top right: SAAB 35FS Draken DK-231 pictured in a climbing turn. Unit markings are not always carried by *Ilmavoimat* aircraft, but this Draken belongs to *Hävittäjälentolaivue 21* (Fighter Squadron 21), organised within the *Satakunnan Lennosto* (Satakunta Wing) at Tampere-Pirkkala AB, which is responsible for airspace surveillance and command/control of interceptors in south-western Finland. Flying components within each *Ilmavoimat* fighter squadron usually comprise two operational Flights with 8-10 Drakens or MiG-21s, one Flight with 4-6 Hawks (for advanced/operational training) and one Flight with single examples of Piper Arrow, Piper Chieftain and Valmet Redigo (for local liaison and communication). (*Jyrki Laukkanen*)

Below right: During March 1991 MiG-21UM MK-105 was repainted in experimental medium/light grey colours, and is seen here cruising in this new scheme. Although giving much better camouflage during flight and when parked on snow-covered ground, the MiG-21 fleet will not be painted in these new colours because of the type's impending replacement by the McDonnell Douglas F/A-18C/D Hornet. (*Jyrki Laukkanen*)

Opposite: *Ilmavoimat* SAAB 35FS Draken DK-231 in a 60 degree climb, appearing in the new toned-down markings introduced during the late 1980s. Powered by a 17,200lb Svenska Flygmotor RM6C afterburning turbofan (licence-produced Rolls-Royce Avon 300 with Swedish-developed afterburner), the Draken is capable of more than Mach 2 at high altitude. Finnish standard air-to-air weaponry includes Swedish-manufactured Rb27/Rb28 Falcon missiles (licence-produced AIM-26B and AIM-4D) and Rb24/Rb74 Sidewinder missiles (licence-produced AIM-9J and AIM-9L). (*Jyrki Laukkanen*)

Below: Named *Kreivi von Rosen* (Count von Rosen) in memory of the Swede who founded military aviation in Finland back in 1918, SAAB 35S Draken DK-223 is operated by *Hävittäjälentolaivue 11* (Fighter Squadron 11), the *Lapin Lennosto* (Lapland Wing) at Rovaniemi AB. Responsible for airspace surveillance as well as command and control of interceptors in northern Finland, this unit is actually situated inside the Arctic Circle and experiences particularly demanding operating conditions during winter with temperatures often as low as minus 35 degrees C. and perpetual darkness most of the time. (*Author*)

Opposite: *Ilmavoimat* SAAB 35FS Draken DK-231 flies straight and level, sporting the toned-down markings introduced during the late 1980s. (*Jyrki Laukkanen*)

Below: A pleasing air-to-air study of a two-seat SAAB 35CS Draken trainer, DK268, as it flies over the 'country of a thousand lakes' which is so beautiful when covered by snow during the winter. *Ilmavoimat* includes five of these ex-*Flygvapnet* SK35C conversion trainers in its inventory and, like in Sweden, they are not camouflaged but have retained the natural metal finish. Completely without operational equipment (no radar, weapons systems or underwing pylons), this relatively light trainer has the highest thrust-to-weight ratio of all Draken versions and is generally regarded as the family sports car. *(Jyrki Laukkanen)*

Opposite: An impressive Draken flight-line during the annual summer shooting camp, where all fighter units deploy to Oulu in Northern Finland for a three-week period to practice air-to-air gunnery against targets towed by Learjets. All single-seat SAAB Draken variants operated by *Ilmavoimat* are visible in this shot, including the 35S (special J35XS export version delivered factory-fresh), 35BS and 35FS (refurbished *Flygvapnet* surplus J35B and J35F versions, respectively). Among Finnish personnel the SAAB Draken is often affectionately referred to as '*Sigurd*'. *(Jyrki Laukkanen)*

Top right: British Aerospace Hawk Mk51 HW-305 of the *Koelentokeskus* (Flight Test Centre) at Halli AB flying inverted on top of a loop high in the Finnish sky. Principal *Ilmavoimat* Hawk operator is the *Koulutuslentolaivue* (Flight Training Squadron) of the *Ilmasotakoulu* (Flying School) at Kauhava AB. Here pilot candidates receive 45 hours of primary flying training on the Valmet Vinka followed by 160 hours intermediate and advanced flying training on the Hawk. Then student pilots are transferred to a front-line unit for operational and tactical flying training on Hawk and Draken or MiG-21. (*Author*)

Below right: A view of the Oulu flight-line during the annual armament practice camp, with a nice line-up of Hawk Mk51 (armed with 30mm gun pod) and MiG-21bis between sorties. Oulu is a civil airfield with military reserve base status, and during a three-week period each summer *Ilmavoimat* fighter squadrons deploy here on an alternating basis to practice air-to-air gunnery against targets towed by Learjets. (*Jyrki Laukkanen*)

Opposite: British Aerospace Hawk Mk51 HW-305 of the *Koelentokeskus* (Flight Test Centre) at Halli AB climbs vertically during a loop high in the Finnish sky. This aircraft is configured with various test equipment, including a special pitot boom. (*Jyrki Laukkanen*)

Below: During early 1991 Hawk HW-344 and MiG-21UM MK-105 were repainted in experimental light-medium grey camouflage, and are seen here in formation clearly showing its effectiveness among clouds and above snow-covered ground. This new colour scheme has been adopted for the Hawk. Seven attrition-replacement Hawk Mk51As ordered for 1993 delivery will arrive in grey camouflage while all other Hawks will be repainted when required during routine maintenance. (*Jyrki Laukkanen*)

Opposite: Potez-Fouga CM170 Magister FM-45 loops for a final picture over snow-covered Finland, before being retired from active *Ilmavoimat* service in December 1988. The Magister had a 30-year long career with *Koulutuslentolaivue* (Flight Training Squadron) at Kauhava, until being replaced by the BAe Hawk Mk51. (*Jyrki Laukkanen*)

Top and below: Three specially modified Gates Learjet 35A/S are operated by the *Kuljetuslentolaivue* (Transport Squadron) at Utti AB for photo-mapping, target-towing and ECM training, having replaced a pair of venerable Ilyushin Il-28R 'Beagles' in these roles. Here LJ-3 is seen flying high in the Finnish sky. (*Jyrki Laukkanen*)

Opposite: *Ilmavoimat* Learjet 35A/S is pictured shortly after take-off from Oulu with sleeve targets deployed, at the start of an air-to-air gunnery target-towing mission during the annual armament practice camp. (*Jyrki Laukkanen*)

Below: RG-1 was the first of 10 Valmet Redigos delivered to *Ilmavoimat* in 1992-93 for local communications flying, and is seen here during acceptance test flights at Halli AB. The name *Haijala* below the windscreen is in memory of the first *Ilmavoimat* pilot who was posthumously promoted to the rank of Flight Master in the late 1930s, shortly after losing his life in an accident. This name has previously been carried by a Valmet Viima and later a Valmet Vihuri trainer. (*Jyrki Laukkanen)*)

Opposite top: Four Piper Arrow IIs are used by different *Ilmavoimat* units for liaison. The PA-2 seen here routing between two air bases belongs to *Hävittäjälentolaivue 21* (Fighter Squadron 21) of the *Satakunnan Lennosto* (Satakunta Wing) at Tampere-Pirkkala. (*Jyrki Laukkanen)*

Opposite bottom: Valmet Vinka VN-10 operated by the *Koulutuslentolaivue* (Fight Training Squadron) of the *Ilmasotakoulu* (Flying School) based at Kauhava is seen undergoing tests with skis on an ice-covered lake in central Finland. (*Jyrki Laukannen)*

Top right: Three Fokker F27 Mk100/400 Friendships form the airlift backbone of the *Kuljetuslentolaivue* (Transport Squadron) fixed-wing flight based at Utti, east of Helsinki. These are the largest aircraft types in *Ilmavoimat* service and the only aircraft regularly seen on visits abroad. (*Author*)

Below right: Piper Chieftain PC-4 of *Hävittäjälentolaivue 31* (Fighter Squadron 31) from the *Karjalan Lennosto* (Karelian Wing) at Kuopio-Rissala is one of six examples of this twin-engined liaison aircraft used by various *Ilmavoimat* units. (*Author*)

Opposite: Mil Mi-8 HS-2 demonstrates its heavy-lift capability during an airshow at Kauhava by moving a Magister as an underslung load. The *Kuljetuslentolaivue* (Transport Squadron) at Utti is using seven of these medium transport helicopters for local liaison as well as Search And Rescue (SAR) missions. Mi-8 helicopters maintain SAR readiness standby at Utti in Southern Finland and at Rovaniemi in northern Finland. (*Jyrki Laukkanen*)

ICELANDIC AIR DEFENCE

The small nation of Iceland is located on a rocky island in the Northern Atlantic between Norway and Greenland, with an area slightly larger than Ireland but with only about 200,000 inhabitants. Some 100 years ago the island was part of the Danish kingdom, but today Iceland is an independent republic. Iceland does not possess any military forces itself, but because of its NATO membership and strategic position the United States has established a large air base at Keflavik.

Resident USAF units at Keflavik include the 56th Air Rescue Squadron (ARS) equipped with Sikorsky MH-60G Pave Hawk helicopters. The 56 ARS maintains a round-the-clock SAR service and has saved more than 250 lives, ranging from local Medevac flights to rescues from sinking ships in the Northern Atlantic. The 57th Fighter Squadron is also based at Keflavik, providing air defence around the island with its McDonnell Douglas F-15C/D Eagles.

Other units keep detachments at Keflavik, including 67th Special Operations Squadron (SOS) from RAF Alconbury with HC-130N/P Hercules tankers (in support of 56 ARS operations) and 552nd Airborne Warning & Control Wing (AWCW) from Tinker AFB, Oklahoma, with E-3B/C Sentry AWACS. Also US Navy patrol squadrons rotate on TDY with Lockheed P-3C Orions.

Opposite: Keflavik also houses a Boeing E-3B/C Sentry detachment from the 552nd Airborne Warning & Control Wing (AWCW) at Tinker AFB in Oklahoma. One of these force multipliers is seen here flying over typical Nordic landscape. (*Peter Foster*)

Below: McDonnell Douglas F-15C Eagle 80-048/IS of 57th Fighter Squadron is towed back to its hangar on a very wet Keflavik AB. The 57th FS reports directly to Air Forces Iceland which is an independent command within the USAF structure. (*Scott van Aken*)

Top right: Winter scenery at Keflavik AB: McDonnell Douglas F-15C Eagle 80-042/IS of 57th Fighter Squadron is parked in the snow at its Icelandic home base. The 57th FS operates in the air defence role above cold and stormy North Atlantic waters between Norway and Greenland. (*Scott van Aken*)

Below right: Lockheed HC-130N Hercules 69-5826 of the 67th Special Operations Squadron (SOS) parked at snow-covered Keflavik. Actually, the 67th SOS is based with 39th Special Operations Wing (SOW) at RAF Alconbury in the UK, but maintains a HC-130N/P detachment at Iceland in support of the 56 ARS which undertake SAR operations from Keflavik with Sikorsky MH-60G Pave Hawk helicopters. (*Scott van Aken*)

ROYAL NORWEGIAN AIR FORCE

As a founder member of NATO, the *Kongelige Norske Luftforsvaret* (Royal Norwegian Air Force) has for many years constituted the northern cornerstone of the Allied defence screen against the East. With a combat element of 5 *Skvadroner* (squadrons) equipped with Northrop F-5 and General Dynamics F-16 fighters, the primary *Luftforsvaret* assignment in NATO strategy has been to prevent the former Soviet forces from bypassing the front line down through the Iceland-Norway gap to attack NATO forces on the central front from behind. However, after the dramatic political changes in Europe in 1991 this Warsaw Pact threat no longer exists.

Because of Norway's special geography (extremely mountainous terrain with many narrow fjords along the coast) *Luftforsvaret* continues to give high priority to its sea invasion defences, including the indigenously developed Penguin Mk3 anti-shipping missile in the F-16A/B's arsenal for this mission. Other maritime roles are performed by P-3 Orion ASW/patrol aircraft and Lynx helicopters operating from *Kystvakten* (Coast Guard) ships of the 'Nordkapp' class.

Luftforsvaret is also tasked with support for the Norwegian Army, with two *Skvadroner* of Bell 412SP Arapaho helicopters transporting land forces between the mountains. Furthermore, the Army itself operates a fleet of Cessna O-1A Bird Dog light aircraft for observation and Forward Air Control (FAC) duties, assigned to the *Feltartilleriets Fly-OP tjeneste* (field artillery air observation post service).

In addition, Norway provides a FOL (Forward Operating Location) for the NATO Airborne Early Warning Force from Geilenkirchen in Germany, with one Boeing E-3A AWACS normally deployed at Ørland Air Base.

Below: A pair of Bodø-based *Skvadron 331* Fighting Falcons armed with Sidewinder AAM training rounds are lined-up for take-off at Ålborg in Denmark. For three weeks every autumn a large contingent of Norwegian F-16s deploys to Danish bases to take part in the local 'Tactical Fighter Weaponry' air exercise. (*Author*)

Below and opposite: F-16B trainer 302 of *Skvadron 332* prepares for a local mission from Rygge. In addition to its primary operational commitments, *Skvadron 332* performs a secondary task of conversion training for all *Luftforsvaret* F-16 pilots in a role comparable to that of RAF Operational Conversion Units. (*Author*)

Below: Four *Skvadron 334* F-16s from Bodø AB line up for take-off during a visit to Bardufoss, the northernmost *Luftforsvaret* base with resident flying units situated some 250km inside the Arctic Circle. Armed with AIM-9L/N Sidewinder missiles and 20mm M-61A Vulcan cannon, Norwegian air defence Falcons are kept on Quick Reaction Alert (QRA) round the clock, intercepting intruders far out over the North Atlantic and Barents Sea. During the mid-1980s, at the height of NATO-WARPAC encounters, *Luftforsvaret* Falcons needed no QRA practice because F-16s were scrambled on more than 400 'live' intercepts of Soviet warplanes each year! (*Author*)

Right: *Skvadron 334's* F-16A is seen flying off the rocky Norwegian coastline armed with the potent NFT fire-and-forget AGM-119B Penguin Mk3 IIR (Imaging InfraRed) anti-shipping missile. *Luftforsvaret* gives high priority to its sea invasion defences because of the special Norwegian geography — any hostile landforce inevitably would run into great difficulties trying to advance through the very mountainous terrain, thus making the many deep fjords along the coastline much more likely assault areas. Purely indigenous and developed by *Norsk Forsvars Teknologi*, the Penguin Mk3 was chosen for the F-16 arsenal after the evaluation of many existing air-to-surface missile types including Exocet, Kormoran, Harpoon and Maverick, all of which failed to function effectively in the narrow fjords confined by steep mountainous slopes. (*Luftforsvaret*)

Below: F-16A of *Skvadron 338*, homebased ot Ørland in central Norway, is about to touch-down during a visit to Rygge AB south of Oslo. All *Luftforsvaret* F-16s will pass through a Mid-Life Update (MLU) modification programme during the 1996-2000 period and are expected to remain in operational service until the year 2020. (*Peter Liander*)

Opposite: F-5A 132 leaves *Skvadron 336's* flight-line; it is the only Norwegian unit still operating the tiny Northrop F-5 Freedom Fighter. All remaining F-5A/Bs have recently received major modifications to extend their service lives well into the 1990s and to improve the type's original avionics. (*Author*)

Top right: F-5A 134 rolls past the *Skvadron 336* flight-line at its home base Rygge. *Skvadron 336* is a true multi-mission squadron, tasked with such diverse roles as local Air Defence (armed with AIM-9 Sidewinder), Electronic Counter Measures (with ALQ-176/*Samovar* jamming pods and A-38N chaff pods), Aggressor training (including Basic Fighter and Dissimilar Air Combat Manoeuvring) and Fighter Lead-in for new pilots. (*Author*)

Below right: *Skvadron 336* at Rygge operates a relatively large number of F-5B two-seaters, including 241 seen here. This is a consequence of roles assigned to the squadron, which includes operational and tactical training of all *Luftforsvaret* fighter pilots arriving from the Euro-NATO Joint Jet Pilot Training Centre at Sheppard AFB in Texas, USA. During the late 1980s removal of this F-5 training phase was tried out, but as a consequence converting new pilots directly onto the more advanced F-16 Fighting Falcon resulted in higher accident rates with operational front-line squadrons. (*Author*)

Opposite: F-5B 136 of *Skvadron 336* from Rygge touches down at Karup in Denmark during an AFNORTH air defence exercise. When operating in the ECM role *Skvadron 336* usually deploys its two-seaters with a special Electronic Tactical Support System operator/navigator in the rear seat. (*Author*)

Below: A close-up of a *Skvadron 336* instructor and student pilot strapping-in for a routine F-5 training mission from Rygge. *Skvadron 336* is a member of the NATO 'Tiger family' and usually visits every Tiger Meet with a couple of aircraft. (*Author*)

Opposite: *Skvadron 335* at Gardermoen outside Oslo operates three Dassault Jet Falcon 20Cs. Two are fitted out for Electronic Warfare (including 053 seen here in new toned-down markings) and one is dressed up as a VIP airplane for transporting members of the Norwegian Royal family, government ministers and high ranking officers from the armed forces. (*Author*)

Below: DA-20C 041 of *Skvadron 335* from Gardermoen lands at Karup in Denmark during the annual 'Tactical Fighter Weaponry' exercise, which Norwegian squadrons usually attend. This Jet Falcon is equipped for Electronic Warfare (EW) and normally operates in support of *Luftforsvaret* F-16 fighters or together with ground-based radars. The EW Jet Falcon also routinely performs calibration of military air navigational aids. (*Author*)

Opposite: The crew of Lockheed P-3B Orion 601 of *Skvadron 333* from Andøya are clearly very proud of their Nordic ancestors, judging from the 'Viking' appearing from the cockpit crew hatch! This P-3B has now been sold to *Ejercito del Aire* (Spanish Air Force) together with four others, and replaced by brand new P-3C Update III Orions. *Skvadron 333* is tasked with primary roles of Maritime Surveillance and Anti-Submarine Warfare as well as a secondary role of Search And Rescue over northern waters. *Luftforsvaret* has named all of its Orions after famous Arctic explorers such as Fridtjof Nansen and Roald Amundsen, reflecting their operational environment. (*Author*)

Below: Hercules 957 of *Skvadron 335* from Gardermoen taxis out for take-off during a visit to Sola Airport. The *Luftforsvaret* C-130 fleet is primarily tasked with troop and cargo transportation within the Norwegian mainland and the islands of Jan Mayen and Svalbard. But *Skvadron 335* also serves as an alert squadron for the United Nations, which has sent its C-130s to many faraway parts of the world, carrying medical equipment and other supplies to the victims of droughts, earthquakes, floods and other natural disasters. (*Author*)

Opposite: *Skvadron 335* Lockheed C-130H Hercules 954 performs an impressive Jet Assisted Take-Off (JATO) during an airshow at Bardufoss. *Skvadron 335* is home based at Gardermoen and operates six C-130H, named *Odin*, *Tor*, *Balder*, *Frøy*, *Ty*, and *Brage*, after ancient Gods from Nordic mythology. (*Author*)

Below: *Skvadron 719* at Bodø operates four de Havilland Canada DHC-6 Twin Otter light transport and communications aircraft, including 057 seen here during a visit to Ørland AB. The 'Twotters' are mainly used in northern Norway, where the type's short-field performance is utilised extensively when flying to many small airfields in the mountainous terrain. (*Author*)

Opposite: Twin Otter 057 of *Skvadron 719* from Bodø is seen during a visit north to Bardufoss, painted in the new two-tone camouflage scheme which recently has replaced the type's older overall-green scheme. Note how the *Luftforsvaret* nationality markings have been toned-down considerably! (*Author*)

Below: The *Luftforsvarets Flygeskole* (Norwegian Air Force Flying School) at Værnes, near Trondheim, is using 18 SAAB MFI-15 Safari primary trainers for grading of pilot candidates and the first 20 hours of basic flying training. Future Norwegian fighter pilots then enter the Euro-NATO Joint Jet Pilot Training Programme in the USA while transport and helicopter pilots are trained by US Navy and US Army flying schools, respectively. (*Author*)

Opposite: Cessna O-1A Bird Dog 2069 is one of 18 operated on behalf of the *Feltartilleriets Fly-OP tjeneste* (field artillery air observation post service) for AOP and FAC duty. The aircraft are peace-time based at Bardufoss in northern Norway and Haslemoen in southern Norway, but in wartime they will be distributed between local Army field formations, each gaining a pair of O-1As. (*Author*)

Below: For many years *Luftforsvaret* has operated a large fleet of Bell UH-1B/C Iroquois utility helicopters mainly in the army support role, although some were also assigned to local SAR duties. The versatile 'Huey' has now been replaced by its larger Bell 412SP brother, but a few UH-1s can still be found in Norway, including 688 seen here with the *Luftforsvarets Tekniske Skole* (Air Force Technical School) at Kjevik. (*Author*)

Opposite: Bell 412SP Arapaho 165 hovers after lift-off from Rygge. *Luftforsvaret* has assigned 18 Arapahos to *Skvadron 339* at Bardufoss AB in Northern Norway and to *Skvadron 720* at Rygge AB in southern Norway, operating in support of Army field manoeuvres. (*Author*)

Top right: Bell 412SP Arapaho 165 hovering after lift-off from Rygge. *Luftforsvaret* has recently introduced extreme toned-down markings to many of its aircraft types, including this utility helicopter. (*Author*)

Below right: *Skvadron 337* at Bardufoss is tasked with fishery protection, oil rig security, maritime patrol and SAR within Norway's extended 200-mile territorial waters, for which six Westland Naval Lynx Mk86 helicopters are regularly flown from the stern platforms of three *Kystvakten* (Coast Guard) ships of the 'Nordkapp' class. Lynx 216 is pictured on a very wet day at its home base. (*Author*)

Opposite: Sea King 189 ready for take-off from Ørland: *Skvadron 330* operates 10 Westland Sea King Mk43 helicopters exclusively in the SAR role, maintaining readiness deployments at the bases of Bodø ('A' Flight), Banak ('B' Flight), Ørland ('C' Flight) and Sola ('D' Flight). (*Author*)

Below: Ørland AB on the Norwegian west coast near Trondheim also provides a Forward Operating Location (FOL) for the NATO Airborne Early Warning Force (NAEWF), with headquarters at Geilenkirchen in Germany. One NAEWF Boeing E-3A AWACS platform is continuously deployed to FOL Ørland on a rotational basis. This approach shot of LX-N90458 clearly shows the 30ft diameter rotodome which houses the Westinghouse AN/APY-2 surveillance radar and IFF/TADIL-C high-speed data link antenna. (*Author*)

SWEDISH AIR FORCE

Without doubt the *Svenska Flygvapnet* (Swedish Air Force) is the largest and most powerful military aviation element within the Nordic countries. This air arm operates some 650-700 fixed wing aircraft and helicopters, organized within 10 *Flygflottiljer* (air wings) and subdivided into 27 *Divisioner* (squadrons). In addition the *Svenska Armén* (Swedish Army) and *Svenska Marinen* (Swedish Navy) operate independent aviation components, mainly equipped with anti-tank, anti-submarine and utility helicopters.

Because of Sweden's longstanding policy of armed neutrality the nation has developed a very competent aviation industry, and through the years the *Svenska Aeroplan Aktiebolaget* (SAAB) has been producing such distinctive fighter designs as the Lansen, Draken, Viggen and Gripen. Sweden today is probably the world's smallest nation still capable of developing and constructing modern multi-role combat aircraft, equal to the most advanced fighters designed and built by the world's largest nations!

Every Swedish fighter design is tailor-made to suit *Flygvapnet's* wartime strategy of highly dispersed operations and this involves combat aircraft deploying to sections of road throughout the country. This requires aircraft designs capable of extreme short-field performance which are also simple to maintain.

Sweden applies its own aircraft type designations, which at first may seem rather confusing but in fact are systematic. All military aircraft have a locally-assigned role prefix and type number, with the roles abbreviated as 'A' for *Attack* (attack), 'J' for *Jakt* (fighter), 'S' for *Spaning* (reconnaissance), 'SK' for *Skol* (training), 'TP' for *Transport* (transport) and 'HKP' for *Helikopter* (helicopter).

Flygvapnet is facing a comprehensive re-equipment and restructuring programme that will replace the older J35 Draken and AJS37 Viggen aircraft with the new JAS39 Gripen and concentrate the number of *Divisioner* within fewer *Flygflottiljer* (air bases closing down include F6 Karlsborg and F13 Norrköping, plus one more).

Below: With its powerful 26,000lb Volvo Flygmotor RM8A bypass engine (a heavily modified licence-built version of the Pratt & Whitney JT8D) in full afterburner, AJ37 Viggen F15-27 of *Hälsinge Flygflottilj* at Söderhamn thunders down the runway on take-off. For several years the Swedish RM8A was the world's most powerful military jet and even from medium altitude it can make the earth shake! To meet requirements for a very short landing performance, the RM8A is equipped with an effective thrust reverser which reduces landing distance to some 500m and can even make the Viggen taxi backwards! (*Author*)

Top right: JA37 Viggen F21-15 of *Norrbottens Flygflottilj* takes off from its home base of Luleå, which is Sweden's northernmost military air base with permanently stationed flying units. Compared to the older tactical Viggens (AJ/SF/SH/SK37 variants), the newer JA37 version is actually a second-generation Viggen optimised for air defence. New systems include the Ericsson PS-46/A pulse Doppler radar and greatly improved avionics, as well as the more powerful RM8B jet engine (28,100lb static thrust) and internal 30mm Oerlikon KCA cannon. (*Peter Foster*)

Below right: JA37 Viggen F16-25 of *Upplands Flygflottilj* from Uppsala north of Stockholm, flies between clouds on a local air defence sortie. When developed by SAAB during the early 1960s the unique Viggen (Thunderbolt) aerodynamic configuration of canard foreplanes and delta-formed main wing was very advanced, but today other aircraft manufacturers have adopted this unconventional geometry for their latest fighter designs. (*Peter Liander*)

Opposite: Newly-modified AJS37 Viggen F6-21 of *Västgöta Flygflottilj* at Karlsborg banks above massive clouds high in the Swedish sky. Presently *Flygvapnet* is converting its older SAAB Viggens of AJ37 attack, SF37 photo-recce and SH37 radar-recce versions into an integrated AJS37 multi-role standard. The 'new' AJS37 is fully operational in attack/recce roles as well as having a limited interceptor capability, although this will be used primarily for self-protection as the second-generation JA37 Viggen version will continue to specialise in air defence. Together with F13 at Norrköping, F6 at Karlsborg is planned to close down by 30 June 1994 as the result of a comprehensive restructuring programme that will make *Flygvapnet* 'meaner, but leaner', as recently expressed by the Swedish Defence Minister. (*Peter Liander*)

Below: All two-seat SK37 operational trainer versions of the SAAB Viggen are operated by *Hälsinge Flygflottilj* at Söderhamn which functions as Viggen conversion unit in addition to its ground-attack role. SK37 Viggen F15-61 parked outside its hangar at Söderhamn clearly displays the extra cockpit which has been positioned behind and slightly above the original cockpit. This has caused a reduction of internal fuel load, and therefore the SK37 always carry the centreline auxiliary drop tank. (*Author*)

Opposite: JA37 Viggen FC-48 of *Försökscentralen* (Test Centre) at Malmslätt is about to touch-down at Söderhamn. *Försökscentralen* is responsible for operational test and development of all Swedish military aircraft and helicopters, including associated avionics and weapons systems, and operates examples of most current *Flygvapnet* types. With the red band round its nose designating test status, FC-48 is one of a few air defence Viggens still painted in the unique tactical splinter camouflage. (*Author*)

Top right: J35F Draken FC-19 of *Försökscentralen* at Malmslätt shortly before touch-down during a visit to Söderhamn. The special bumper tail-wheel was made necessary early in the Draken's service history, when an engine modification increased the afterburner length. The tail-wheel assembly is retractable into its own well in concert with the main landing gear and the tyres are non-inflatable hard rubber. (*Author*)

Below right: J35F F10-66 of *Skånska Flygflottilj* with specially-painted tail-fin displaying the ghost squadron insignia of *1st Division* from *Flygflottilj 10* at Ängelholm. (*Author*)

Opposite: Very nice air-to-air study of two newly-modified all-grey J35J Drakens of *Skånska Flygflottilj* flying high above massive clouds. To extend the operational life of its remaining Draken fleet well into the 1990s, *Flygvapnet* has recently updated a large number of J35Fs, known as the '*Filip*', into a new J35J '*Johan*' version. This modification and refurbishment programme included structural life-time extension, improved Ericsson PS-011 radar reinforced against enemy ECM, an undernose Hughes IR scanner more effective at low level, various updated avionics, two additional underwing pylons and provision for the more effective Rb74 dogfight missile (AIM-9L Sidewinder). (*Peter Liander*)

Top right: *Skånska Flygflottilj* two-seat SK35C Draken trainer F10-82 taxis out for take-off from its home base of Ängelholm. Also known as '*Cäsar*', the SK35C has no operational capability whatsoever, but is a pure tandem trainer with radar, cannon and underwing pylons removed. *Flygvapnet* requirements for new Draken 'drivers' is on average five to 10 pilots per year, but in addition Austrian pilots receive SAAB Draken training at Ängelholm (which Sweden is committed to provide under the contract signed in 1985 when Austria purchased 24 refurbished J350E fighters). (*Author*)

Below right: An impressive line-up of J35F Drakens (Dragon) of *Skånska Flygflottilj* at their Ängelholm base. This is the last unit operating the SAAB Draken in Sweden. (*Peter Liander*)

Opposite: This J35F flying inverted in full afterburner clearly shows the Draken's characteristic double-delta wing configuration. Developed by SAAB during the 1950s, this unique geometry combined good high-speed performance at altitude (Mach 2+) with exceptional low-speed manoeuvrability for short take-off and landing distances (about 500 metres). A not so attractive feature of the double-delta concept was the so-called Superstall phenomenon, a violent and uncontrolled stall starting with the nose oscillating up and down at reduced airspeed but quickly developing into the aircraft falling vertically towards the ground in a stable position with no forward speed at all. Today, the recommended Superstall recovery procedure is to avoid getting into it in the first place. (*Author*)

Below: J32E Lansen F13-03 of *Målflygdivision* (Target Flying Squadron) at Malmslätt, which is part of the Viggen-equipped *Bråvalla Flygflottilj* at nearby Norrköping. *Målflygdivision* is the last unit flying the SAAB Lansen, and operates some 20 modified aircraft in the target-towing and ECM training roles. (*Author*)

Opposite: *Målflygdivision* J32E Lansen F13-07 cruises above a typical mid-Swedish landscape, not far from its home base at Malmslätt. Since first flown on 3 November 1952, the SAAB Lansen has been very popular with *Flygvapnet* pilots because of its easy handling and beautifully clean lines. With no immediate replacement likely, the J32E 'Stör-Lansen' (Jammer Lansen) will continue to operate into the next decade, giving a basic service life of 50 years for this remarkable jet! (*Anders Nylén*)

Below: In addition to its primary flying training commitment, the *Flygflottilj 5* at Ljungbyhed also maintains the *Flygvapnet* aerobatic group, 'Team 60', with one of their six SK60s seen here landing at Söderhamn following a successful display. Today the *Krigsflygskolan* (Military Aviation School) at Ljungbyhed gives new pilot candidates a 125-hour all-jet basic flying training course on the SAAB 105, with the previous piston-engine introductory course on SK61 Bulldogs having been abandoned since 1988. (*Author*)

Opposite: The basic SAAB 105 airframe is operated by *Flygvapnet* in five different variants, including the SK60A two-seat flying trainer, SK60B attack/trainer with six underwing weapons stations, SK60C attack/recce with nose-mounted 35mm KB-18 panoramic camera and IR seeker, and SK60D/E four-seat liaison/utility aircraft, the latter ironically nicknamed '*Jumbo*'. The 'C' version features a characteristic extended nose, as can be seen on this picture of a pair of SK60Cs flying low over a snow-covered landscape. (*Peter Liander*)

Below: One of two Rockwell TP86 Sabreliners operated by *Försökscentralen* (Test Centre) at Malmslätt AB for ECM training and various radar trials, including SAR (Synthetic Aperture Radar) with two arrays dragged behind the aircraft. (*Author*)

Opposite: Scottish Aviation SK61 Bulldog F5-18 is pictured flying over southern Sweden near its Ljungbyhed base. The SK61 was used by *Krigsflygskolan* for basic flying training until 1988, where the school skipped the piston-engine course and adopted an all-jet syllabus on the SAAB 105 jet trainer. Instead, the SK61s are now used for liaison duty at most *Flygvapnet* bases, but *Flygflottilj 5* continues to provide maintenance facilities for the entire Bulldog fleet at Ljungbyhed. (*Peter Liander*)

Top right: A line-up of Bulldogs belonging to *Arméflygbataljon 2* (Army Flying Battalion 2) at Malmslätt. The *Armén* (Swedish Army) Bulldogs are designated FPL61C and some 20 served in AOP and FAC roles until recently when *Armén* stopped fixed-wing operations and became an all-helicopter force. (*Author*)

Below right: A line-up of SK50 Safirs at Halmstad. With deliveries to *Flygvapnet* having started back in 1953, the Safir was used at Ljungbyhed for basic flying training for some 20 years, before being transferred to local liaison duty. (*Author*)

Opposite: A pleasing air-to-air study of a nine-ship SAAB 91B/C Safir liaison aircraft formation, designated SK50 in *Flygvapnet* service. Until recently every *Flygflottilj* had a handful of SK50 Safirs at their disposal for local liaison and utility flying, but now the SK61 Bulldogs previously used by the *Krigsflygskolan* have taken over this role. (*Anders Nylén*)

Below: Three Beech TP101 Super King Airs are operated by *Flygvapnet* for personnel and light transport flights, with one assigned to each of the *Flygflottiljer* at Såtenäs, Ronneby and Luleå. F7-011, seen here, crashed during landing on 24 September 1990 but has been replaced by another example. (*Author*)

Opposite: Lockheed C-130H Hercules F7-843 takes off with its four Allison T56-A-15 turboprops at full power. The Swedes have designated the Hercules TP84, and eight examples are operated by the *Transport-flygdivision* (Transport Squadron) of *Skaraborgs Flygflottilj* at Såtenäs. (*Peter Foster*)

Below: The *Flygvapnet* SAR helicopter fleet still includes a few Agusta-Bell 204B Iroquois, designated as HKP3B. Luleå-based F21-86 of *Norrbottens Flygflottilj* rests between missions on the special tow-wagon on which the helicopter lands for ground transport. *(Christoph Kugler)*

Opposite: A dozen HKP3C (AB204B Iroquois) helicopters are operated by the *Armén* (Swedish Army) in the utility and battlefield liaison roles. Most are operated by *Arméflygbataljon 1* at Boden, near Luleå, like this example parked in a local field. *(Author)*

Below: *Marinen* (Swedish Navy) Boeing-Vertol/ Kawasaki 107, designated as HKP4B/C, hovers after lift-off from its Säve base. This large rotorcraft is operated by three *Helikopterdivisioner*, No11 at Berga (Stockholm), No12 at Säve (Göteborg) and No13 at Kallinge (Ronneby), all tasked with ASW and SAR around Sweden's extensive coastline. (*Author*)

Right: A three-ship flight of *Marinen* HKP4B/C helicopters on patrol low over Swedish waters (note how the distinctive splinter camouflage is applied even to the rotor blades). Since the famous 'Whisky on the Rocks' incident in October 1981, when Soviet 'Whisky' class submarine No137 ran aground in a restricted military zone only 15km from the Swedish naval base complex in Karlskrona, *Marinen* ASW capability has been boosted considerably to prevent foreign U-boats from prowling Swedish waters more or less at will. Thus the BV/KV-107 fleet has been increased with surplus *Flygvapnet* HKP4A examples and updated with advanced anti-submarine weapons systems. (*Thorbjörn Olsen*)

Below: Hughes 300C line-up at Malmslätt, where *Arméflygbataljon 2* (Army Flying Battalion 2) undertakes basic helicopter flying training for all Swedish Army, Navy and Air Force helo-pilot candidates with these small helicopters, designated as HKP5B. (*Author*)

Opposite: *Marinen* also operates a number of AB206A Jet Ranger utility helicopters, with the Swedish designation HKP6B. This example from *Helikopterdivision 12* is hovering at its Säve home base outside Göteborg on the Swedish west coast. The Jet Ranger can be armed with lightweight torpedoes and depth charges to supplement the larger and more capable Vertol 107 in the ASW role. (*Author*)

Top right: A pair of *Armén* HKP6A (Agusta-Bell 206A Jet Ranger) from *Armé-flygbataljon 1* at Boden rest between sorties during a field exercise in northern Sweden. (*Author*)

Below right: F6-93 is one of four MBB BO 105CBS SAR helicopters included in the *Flygvapnet* inventory with the designation HKP9B. They are tasked with SAR over the large Vänern and Vättern lakes and operated by *Helikoptergruppen* (Helicopter Groups) at Karlsborg and Såtenäs. (*Author*)

Opposite: Newly-delivered HKP10 Super Puma F15-95 from the *Helikoptergrupp* at Söderhamn flies along a typical piece of Swedish coastline. During 1988-90, 10 Aérospatiale AS332Ms were delivered to the SAR flights of F7, F15, F17 and F21 as replacement for the almost 30-year-old Vertol 107, of which four have been passed on to *Marinen* and the rest placed in storage. (*Peter Liander*)

Below: Atmospheric shot of the General Dynamics
F-16A Fighting Falcon cruising against a beautiful
sunset backdrop. (*Flyvevåbnet*)